D0811303
201721728 U

WHO ELSE writes like ?

A Readers' Guide to Fiction Authors

Compiled and
edited by Roy Huse

LISU
Loughborough University of Technology
1993

First published as: MANN, Peter H.

A Readers' Guide to Fiction Authors
Loughborough University, 1985.

This sequel compiled and edited by Roy Huse, 1993.

Published by the Library and Information Statistics Unit (LISU),
Department of Information and Library Studies,
Loughborough University of Technology, Loughborough, LE11 3TU

British Library Cataloguing in Publication Data may be obtained from the British Library

ISBN 0 948848 47 2

Cover design by Susan England

Printed and bound in Great Britain by Butler & Tanner Ltd
Frome, Somerset

CONTENTS

INTRODUCTION

The first edition of 'The Readers' Guide to Fiction Authors' was published in 1985. Compiled by Peter Mann it set out to answer one of the most frequent questions from public library users... "Who writes like my favourite author?" The first edition was based on a list of 61 'Core' authors to which were added alternatives compiled from names submitted by over 600 librarians. Since the Guide was published we have had access to the statistics collected by the Registrar of Public Lending Right which provide us with the names of those authors whose works are most often borrowed from Public Libraries - a unique opportunity to see who really *are* the 'Top of the Pops'.

This new edition of **The Readers' Guide**, while following the successful arrangement of the first edition, is almost entirely a new compilation. It is based principally, but not exclusively, on the most popular authors from recent Public Lending Right lists to which a number of professional librarians and fiction specialists have added other names and alternative authors whose genre and writing style are similar. All the entries in the main alphabetical section have been cross referenced through the use of Hypertext.

The development of a Hypertext version of this book allowed links between authors and the spelling of authors' names to be checked very rapidly. It also helped in the process of adding genres to authors, and was used to create the genre index. The Hypertext version is an exciting utility in its own right, and is capable of being developed into a facility for searching on CD-ROMs and OPACs. It could be produced as a self-contained electronic Reader's Guide for use in libraries.

The majority of authors listed are currently popular in Public Libraries throughout the United Kingdom. Older favourites and classic writers are not included but there are alternative guides to help and these are listed in the **Bibliography** at the end of the book.

Of course no one author writes exactly like another; indeed everyone's creative work is unique. However there is often sufficient similarity within a style or a content to link the novels of one author with those of another. Within this Guide over 1,000 novelists are listed, some of whose names may be new to you.

There are three further features. Many authors write exclusively within a category or genre. Where they do so this is indicated under their name in the main text but also under the **Authors Listed by Genre** section so that you may find all the writers of one category brought together. There is a list of **Literary Prizes and Awards** together with the names of recent winners.

Finally a short **Bibliography** to cover current guides has also been included as a further aid to widen your fiction horizons.

Who Else Writes Like...? A Readers' Guide to Fiction Authors has been published to assist readers and library staff explore the exciting world of contemporary fiction. Inevitably there will be disagreement with some suggestions, but the book has been compiled conscientiously from the collective experience of many Librarians.

Although Copyright remains with the British Library there is no restriction on using appropriate parts of the Guide to promote a greater awareness of the wide range of fiction available to Library users.

It is hoped to produce another edition in 2-3 years, so if you have any constructive comments please send them to the publisher, the Director of LISU, Loughborough University of Technology, Loughborough, Leicestershire, LE11 3TU.

ACKNOWLEDGEMENTS

This Guide could not have been produced without the active support of many Library Authorities and their staff who have willingly given a great deal of their time and professional expertise to the compilation of the lists of authors. Other organisations including one major library supplier together with a number of individuals have all made significant contributions towards the task of compiling and editing the text. Whilst it is not possible to name everyone individually I am particularly grateful to the following Library Authorities, to the individual members of staff named and to their colleagues who helped in the task. I hope they will be pleased with the result.

ANGUS LIBRARIES, especially John Doherty, John MacRitchie and the staff of Kirriemuir Library
BROMLEY LIBRARIES - Ruth Alston and colleagues
BUCKINGHAMSHIRE COUNTY LIBRARY - Jenny Varney and colleagues
CALDERDALE LIBRARIES - Chris Kearns
CHESHIRE COUNTY LIBRARY - L.P. Morgan and colleagues
CLYDEBANK DISTRICT LIBRARIES, especially Ian Baillie
DORSET COUNTY LIBRARY - Bryan Evans and colleagues
EAST SUSSEX COUNTY LIBRARY - Barry Foster and colleagues
EALING LIBRARIES - Peter and Frances Hounsell; Brian and Yvonne Cope
GWENT COUNTY LIBRARY - Sue Johnson and colleagues
HAMPSHIRE COUNTY LIBRARY - Barrie Kempthorne and colleagues
HEREFORD AND WORCESTER COUNTY LIBRARY - Frances Yeats and colleagues
HERTFORDSHIRE LIBRARIES - Heidi Ebrahim, Bob Sharpe and colleagues
LEEDS CITY LIBRARIES - Lionel Aldridge and Judith Rhodes
SOUTH EAST EDUCATION AND LIBRARY BOARD - J.H. Marshall, Joan Barfoot and Sam McDowell
SUFFOLK ARTS AND LIBRARIES - Richard Attenborrow and Jenny Salisbury; Vincent McDonald and colleagues
WEST SUSSEX COUNTY LIBRARY - especially Margaret Hampson

Individuals who have suggested authors' names, usually within a specialised field, include Geoffrey Paterson, Andy Sawyer (British Science Fiction Association) and Frances Whitehead (Mills and Boon). A special thank you to Duncan Turner and James Askew & Son for their wholehearted support for the project and for the contribution made by Dennis Kelly to the author lists.

I am grateful to the Registrar of Public Lending Right for permission to use his statistics as the basis for the core list of authors and to Cambridgeshire Libraries who supplied details of their genre authors which helped in compiling the categories used in this Guide. My thanks also to the various organisations who supplied information for the list of Literary Prizes and Awards.

I have received consistent support and encouragement from my publisher - John Sumsion, Director of LISU, and also from the Editorial Board - which includes among its members Peter Mann whose idea it was to produce the original guide.

A small team working on the project has included Richard Marriott who did much of the early market testing and Robert Clayton whose research and use of computer programs has been invaluable. Mary Ashworth and Sharon Fletcher, with the assistance of Kate Dexter, have been mainly responsible for the typesetting and early production work as well as ensuring good communication between Loughborough and Aldwick. Their work has been invaluable.

Finally my thanks go to my wife Jeanne who has given me constant support and encouragement as well as spending many hours on detailed research in addition to typing the lists ready for transmission to Loughborough.

Roy Huse
Aldwick September 1993

HOW TO USE THIS GUIDE

The arrangement is very simple. Look up the author you want in the Alphabetical List The names which follow are suggested alternatives. For example: if you like Margaret FORSTER you might also enjoy books by Margaret DRABBLE or Deborah MOGGACH. There is no guarantee that you will, but they are authors who usually write in a similar style.

Where an author writes in a category or genre this is indicated. The alternative authors which then follow usually write in a similar genre. For example Ted ALLBEURY usually writes *Adventure* or *Spy Stories* and this is shown by the word *Adventure* under his name.

Sometimes an author writes under the same name but in two quite different genres. We have shown the alternatives under the two headings: For example Evelyn ANTHONY *(Adventure)* and Evelyn ANTHONY *(Historical).*

Do remember that some authors who write frequently in one category will occasionally produce a book in a quite different genre. It is important to read the jacket details or summary of the book before you borrow.

If you only want a list of authors who write in a particular category or genre then turn straight to page 179.

Novels which have been awarded a **Literary Prize** are sometimes overlooked when the initial publicity has subsided. The lists beginning on page 205 will help you trace the winners in recent years.

There are many other guides and lists which will also help you explore the world of fiction or assist you in finding the book or series you want. A selection is listed in the **Bibliography** on page 237.

This Guide is not infallible but it is easy to use. If you need more information library staff are there to help.

THE READERS' GUIDE: AN ALPHABETICAL LIST

Peter ABRAHAMS
War

W.E.B. GRIFFIN
John HARRIS
Derek ROBINSON
Terence STRONG

Chinua ACHEBE
General

James BALDWIN
Saul BELLOW
J.M. COETZEE
V.S. NAIPAUL
Ben OKRI
Isaac Bashevis SINGER

Peter ACKROYD
General

John BANVILLE
Julian BARNES
Anthony BURGESS
A.S. BYATT
Peter CAREY
J.G. FARRELL
John FOWLES
Robert NYE
Graham SWIFT
Barry UNSWORTH

Douglas ADAMS
Science Fiction

Ben ELTON
Michael FRAYN
Harry HARRISON
Tom HOLT
Grant NAYLOR
Terry PRATCHETT
Robert RANKIN
Bob SHAW
Robert SHECKLEY

Richard ADAMS
General

Aeron CLEMENT
Paul GALLICO
William HORWOOD
A.R. LLOYD
Henry WILLIAMSON

Robert ADAMS
Fantasy

David EDDINGS
Tom HOLT
Stephen LAWS
A.R. LLOYD
Mary STANTON

Elizabeth ADLER
Family Stories

Barbara Taylor BRADFORD

Brenda JAGGER

Janet TANNER

Elizabeth VILLARS

Joan AIKEN
General

Margaret DRABBLE

Clare HARKNESS

Elizabeth HARRIS

Georgette HEYER

Susan HILL

Mary STEWART

Catherine AIRD
Crime

Margery ALLINGHAM

Simon BRETT

W.J. BURLEY

Agatha CHRISTIE

Elizabeth FERRARS

Patricia WENTWORTH

Margaret YORKE

Brian W. ALDISS
Science Fiction

Isaac ASIMOV

J.G. BALLARD

Ray BRADBURY

David BRIN

Richard COWPER

Harry HARRISON

Robert A. HEINLEIN

Frank HERBERT

Brian STABLEFORD

John WYNDHAM

Ted ALLBEURY
Adventure

Eric AMBLER

Evelyn ANTHONY

Tom CLANCY

Clive EGLETON

Ken FOLLETT

Colin FORBES

Frederick FORSYTH

Brian FREEMANTLE

Adam HALL

Palma HARCOURT

Robert LUDLUM

Helen MACINNES

Tim SEBASTIAN

Gerald SEYMOUR

Charlotte Vale ALLEN
Family Stories

Betty BURTON

Josephine COX

Janet DAILEY

Cynthia FREEMAN

Claire LORRIMER

Pamela OLDFIELD

Danielle STEEL

Jessica STEELE

Nicola THORNE

Helen VAN SLYKE

Patricia MOYES

Dorothy L. SAYERS

Joan SMITH

Josephine TEY

Patricia WENTWORTH

Isabel ALLENDE
General

Margaret ATWOOD

Günter GRASS

Milan KUNDERA

Margery ALLINGHAM
Crime

Catherine AIRD

Nicholas BLAKE

Gwendoline BUTLER

Edmund CRISPIN

Freeman Wills CROFTS

Lesley GRANT-ADAMSON

Georgette HEYER

Michael INNES

P.D. JAMES

Emma LATHEN

Ngaio MARSH

Gladys MITCHELL

Gwen MOFFAT

Lisa ALTHER
General

Ethan CANIN

Marilyn FRENCH

Alice HOFFMAN

Toni MORRISON

Ann OAKLEY

Judith ROSSNER

Anne TYLER

Eric AMBLER
Adventure

Ted ALLBEURY

John BUCHAN

Victor CANNING

Peter DRISCOLL

Ian FLEMING

John GARDNER

Adam HALL

Palma HARCOURT

Hammond INNES

Robert LITTELL

Wilbur SMITH

Kingsley AMIS
General

William BOYD

Malcolm BRADBURY

John BRAINE

William COOPER

Robertson DAVIES

Lawrence DURRELL

Ben ELTON

Michael FRAYN

David LODGE

Stanley MIDDLETON

David NOBBS

Piers Paul READ

Tom SHARPE

Alan SILLITOE

Leslie THOMAS

Peter TINNISWOOD

Keith WATERHOUSE

Evelyn WAUGH

A.N. WILSON

Martin AMIS
General

Julian BARNES

William BOYD

Malcolm BRADBURY

Roddy DOYLE

David LODGE

Ian McEWAN

Brian MOORE

John UPDIKE

Valerie ANAND
Historical

Philippa CARR

Dorothy DUNNETT

Morgan LLYWELYN

Edith PARGETER

Jean PLAIDY

Poul ANDERSON
Science Fiction

Isaac ASIMOV

Robert BLOCH

Ray BRADBURY

David BRIN

Jack L. CHALKER

Gordon R. DICKSON

Harlan ELLISON

Joe HALDEMAN

Fred SABERHAGEN

Robert SILVERBERG

Gene WOLFE

Roger ZELAZNY

Lucilla ANDREWS
Romance

Iris BROMIGE

Barbara CARTLAND

Marion CHESNEY

Anne MATHER

Claire RAYNER

Denise ROBINS

Patricia ROBINS

Elizabeth SEIFERT

D.E. STEVENSON

Lyn ANDREWS
Family Stories

Kate FLYNN

Helen FORRESTER

Sara FRASER

Frances PAIGE

Sarah SHEARS

Virginia ANDREWS
General

Virginia COFFMAN

Suzanne GOODWIN

Sheelagh KELLY

Barbara MICHAELS

Daoma WINSTON

Patricia ANGADI
General

Lynne Reid BANKS

Anita BROOKNER

Deborah MOGGACH

Bernice RUBENS

Mary WESLEY

Evelyn ANTHONY
Adventure

Ted ALLBEURY

Colin FORBES

Clare FRANCIS

Palma HARCOURT

Helen MACINNES

Gerald SEYMOUR

Evelyn ANTHONY
Historical

Barbara ERSKINE

Catherine GAVIN

Cynthia HARROD-EAGLES

Genevieve LYONS

Diana NORMAN

Jean PLAIDY

Philippa WIAT

Piers ANTHONY
Science Fiction

Greg BEAR
Jack L. CHALKER
Philip Jose FARMER
Alan Dean FOSTER
Terry PRATCHETT

Jeffrey ARCHER
Adventure

Michael DOBBS
Ken FOLLETT
John GARDNER
Robert GODDARD
William HAGGARD
Arthur HAILEY
Gerald SEYMOUR
Sidney SHELDON
John TRENHAILE

Campbell ARMSTRONG
Adventure

Colin FORBES
Reginald HILL
Julian Jay SAVARIN
Craig THOMAS
John TRENHAILE

Lindsay ARMSTRONG
Romance

Penny JORDAN
Rosemary HAMMOND
Carole MORTIMER
Annabel MURRAY
Anne WEALE

Thomas ARMSTRONG
Family Stories

Phyllis BENTLEY
Taylor CALDWELL
A.J. CRONIN
Mazo DE LA ROCHE
R.F. DELDERFIELD
J.B. PRIESTLEY
Howard SPRING
Marguerite STEEN

Isaac ASIMOV
Science Fiction

Brian W. ALDISS
Poul ANDERSON
James BLISH
Arthur C. CLARKE
Philip K. DICK
Joe HALDEMAN
Harry HARRISON
Robert A. HEINLEIN
Frank HERBERT

Michael MOORCOCK

Larry NIVEN

Frederik POHL

Fred SABERHAGEN

Bob SHAW

Clifford D. SIMAK

Brian STABLEFORD

Roger ZELAZNY

Robert ASPRIN
Fantasy

Dan McGIRT

Terry PRATCHETT

Robert RANKIN

Christopher STASHEFF

Margaret ATWOOD
General

Isabel ALLENDE

Pat BARKER

A.S. BYATT

Barbara COMYNS

Anita DESAI

Janice ELLIOTT

Nadine GORDIMER

Ruth Prawer JHABVALA

Iris MURDOCH

Carol SHIELDS

Muriel SPARK

Anne TYLER

Fay WELDON

Virginia WOOLF

Jean M. AUEL
Fantasy

Stephen DONALDSON

Nicholas LUARD

Elizabeth M. THOMAS

Jonathan AYCLIFFE
Supernatural

James HERBERT

Peter JAMES

Stephen KING

Dean R. KOONTZ

Robert McCAMMON

Peter STRAUB

Marian BABSON
Crime

Simon BRETT

Pat BURDEN

Agatha CHRISTIE

Elizabeth FERRARS

Elizabeth LEMARCHAND

Magdalen NABB

Simon SHAW

Neville STEED

Desmond BAGLEY
Adventure

Victor CANNING

Jon CLEARY

Clive CUSSLER

Nelson DE MILLE

Ken FOLLETT

Clare FRANCIS

Alexander FULLERTON

John GARDNER

Robert GODDARD

Arthur HAILEY

Jack HIGGINS

Hammond INNES

Geoffrey JENKINS

Duncan KYLE

James LEASOR

Helen MACINNES

Alistair MACLEAN

Gerald SEYMOUR

Nevil SHUTE

Wilbur SMITH

Craig THOMAS

Hilary BAILEY
General

Nina BAWDEN

Alice Thomas ELLIS

Jane GARDAM

Hilary MANTEL

Paul BAILEY
General

David COOK

Mervyn JONES

Ian McEWAN

Brian MOORE

Piers Paul READ

Beryl BAINBRIDGE
General

Lynne Reid BANKS

Jenny DISKI

Margaret DRABBLE

Alice Thomas ELLIS

Penelope FITZGERALD

Margaret FORSTER

Susan HILL

Elizabeth Jane HOWARD

Jennifer JOHNSTON

Doris LESSING

Ian McEWAN

Shena MACKAY

Penelope MORTIMER

Wendy PERRIAM

Bernice RUBENS

Margery SHARP

Muriel SPARK

Fay WELDON

James BALDWIN
General

Chinua ACHEBE

Toni MORRISON

Alan PATON

Alice WALKER

John Edgar WIDEMAN

Richard WRIGHT

J.G. BALLARD
Science Fiction

Brian ALDISS

Iain M. BANKS

Ray BRADBURY

Anthony BURGESS

Philip K. DICK

Christopher PRIEST

Ian WATSON

John WYNDHAM

Iain M. BANKS
Science Fiction

J.G. BALLARD

Ray BRADBURY

Ian WATSON

John WYNDHAM

Lynne Reid BANKS
General

Patricia ANGADI

Beryl BAINBRIDGE

Monica DICKENS

Margaret DRABBLE

Nadine GORDIMER

Olivia MANNING

Edna O'BRIEN

Muriel SPARK

Anne TYLER

Russell BANKS
General

Shusako ENDO

Kazuo ISHIGURO

Yukio MISHIMA

Haruki MURAKAMI

John BANVILLE
General

Peter ACKROYD

Peter CAREY

John McGAHERN

Bernard MACLAVERTY

Barry UNSWORTH

Noel BARBER
General

Dirk BOGARDE

Jon CLEARY

R.F. DELDERFIELD

Malcolm MACDONALD

James A. MICHENER

Janet TANNER

Tessa BARCLAY
Family Stories

Emma BLAIR

Betty BURTON

Catherine COOKSON

Elizabeth DAISH

Margaret Thomson DAVIS

Rosemary ENRIGHT

Audrey HOWARD

Brenda JAGGER

Marie JOSEPH

Claire LORRIMER

Anne MELVILLE

Maisie MOSCO

Pamela OLDFIELD

Denise ROBERTSON

Susan SALLIS

Jessica STIRLING

Reay TANNAHILL

Nicola THORNE

A.L. BARKER
General

Anita BROOKNER

Barbara PYM

Emma TENNANT

Clive BARKER
Fantasy

Jamie DELANO

Neil GAIMAN

Dave GIBBONS

Stephen KING

Robert McCAMMON

Alan MOORE

John WAGNER

Pat BARKER
General

Margaret ATWOOD

Stan BARSTOW

Janice ELLIOTT

Anne TYLER

Robert BARNARD
Crime

Simon BRETT

Colin DEXTER

Jonathan GASH

John HARVEY

Mark HEBDEN

Michael TOLKIN

Michael UNDERWOOD

Julian BARNES
General

Peter ACKROYD

Martin AMIS

William BOYD

Bruce CHATWIN

Sebastian FAULKS

Kazuo ISHIGURO

Patrick McCABE

Ian McEWAN

Paul MICOU

Timothy MO

Brian MOORE

Graham SWIFT

D.M. THOMAS

A.N. WILSON

Linda BARNES
Crime

Liza CODY

Amanda CROSS

Frances FYFIELD

Sue GRAFTON

Susan MOODY

Sara PARETSKY

Stan BARSTOW
General

Pat BARKER

H.E. BATES

Malcolm BRADBURY

Melvyn BRAGG

John BRAINE

Mervyn JONES

D.H. LAWRENCE

Stanley MIDDLETON

Alan SILLITOE

Howard SPRING

David STOREY

Ronald BASSETT
Sea

Alan EVANS

Porter HILL

Alexander KENT

Philip McCUTCHAN

Patrick O'BRIAN

Douglas REEMAN

Anthony TREW

Richard WOODMAN

H.E. BATES
General

Stan BARSTOW

Melvyn BRAGG

A.J. CRONIN

H.E. BATES (cont.)

Robertson DAVIES
R.F. DELDERFIELD
Monica DICKENS
Paul GALLICO
L.P. HARTLEY
Miss READ
Nevil SHUTE
Howard SPRING
Denys VAL BAKER

H.E. BATES
Humour

E.F. BENSON
George Macdonald FRASER
Richard GORDON
Tom HOLT
Garrison KEILLOR
David NOBBS
Peter TINNISWOOD
Keith WATERHOUSE

Nina BAWDEN
General

Hilary BAILEY
Phyllis BENTLEY
Monica DICKENS
Margaret DRABBLE
Margaret FORSTER
Nadine GORDIMER
Georgina HAMMICK
Penelope LIVELY
Alison LURIE
Muriel SPARK
Joanna TROLLOPE
Mary WESLEY

William BAYER
Crime

James Lee BURKE
Loren D. ESTLEMAN
Dashiell HAMMETT
Elmore LEONARD
David L. LINDSEY
John SANDFORD

Greg BEAR
Science Fiction

Piers ANTHONY
C.J. CHERRYH
Arthur C. CLARKE
Philip Jose FARMER
James P. HOGAN
Frederik POHL
Bob SHAW

Sally BEAUMAN
The 'Smart Set'

Julie BURCHILL

Jackie COLLINS

Jilly COOPER

Elizabeth GAGE

Burt HIRSCHFELD

Molly PARKIN

Harold ROBBINS

Jacqueline SUSANN

Josephine BELL
Crime

Agatha CHRISTIE

Ngaio MARSH

Joyce PORTER

C.F. ROE

Dorothy L. SAYERS

Simon BELL
General

Richard CONDON

Michael CRICHTON

Robin COOK

Mario PUZO

Guy BELLAMY
Humour

Roddy DOYLE

Michael FRAYN

David NOBBS

Tom SHARPE

Peter TINNISWOOD

Pamela BELLE
Historical

Philippa CARR

Emma DRUMMOND

Dorothy DUNNETT

Cynthia HARROD-EAGLES

Rosalind LAKER

Anya SETON

Saul BELLOW
General

Chinua ACHEBE

Andre BRINK

Anthony BURGESS

Howard FAST

William FAULKNER

E.M. FORSTER

John FOWLES

Joseph HELLER

Herman HESSE

James JOYCE

Primo LEVI

Norman MAILER

Brian MOORE

Vladimir NABOKOV

V.S. NAIPAUL

Saul BELLOW (cont.)

John O'HARA

Philip ROTH

Isaac Bashevis SINGER

William STYRON

Paul THEROUX

John UPDIKE

Leon URIS

Morris WEST

E.F. BENSON
Humour

H.E. BATES

Henry CECIL

Richard GORDON

A.G. MACDONELL

Angela THIRKELL

Evelyn WAUGH

P.G. WODEHOUSE

Phyllis BENTLEY
General

Thomas ARMSTRONG

Nina BAWDEN

Elizabeth BOWEN

Taylor CALDWELL

A.J. CRONIN

R.F. DELDERFIELD

Dorothy EDEN

John GALSWORTHY

Elizabeth GOUDGE

Winifred HOLTBY

Richard LLEWELLYN

J.B. PRIESTLEY

Howard SPRING

Rachel BILLINGTON
General

Rosemary FRIEDMAN

Elizabeth Jane HOWARD

Penelope LIVELY

Alison LURIE

Olivia MANNING

Gillian TINDALL

Maeve BINCHY
Family Stories

Clare BOYLAN

Kathleen CONLON

Frank DELANEY

Sarah HARRISON

Audrey HOWARD

Elizabeth Jane HOWARD

Molly KEANE

Sheelagh KELLY

Beryl KINGSTON

Edna O'BRIEN

Rosamunde PILCHER

Erin PIZZEY

Belva PLAIN

Deirdre PURCELL
Elvi RHODES
Janet TANNER

Emma BLAIR
Family Stories

Tessa BARCLAY
Harry BOWLING
Catherine COOKSON
Margaret Thomson DAVIS
Helen FORRESTER
Christine Marion FRASER
Cynthia FREEMAN
Audrey HOWARD
Brenda JAGGER
Marie JOSEPH
Sheelagh KELLY
Lena KENNEDY
Beryl KINGSTON
Claire LORRIMER
Elisabeth McNEILL
Pamela OLDFIELD
Elvi RHODES
Denise ROBERTSON
Jessica STIRLING
Nicola THORNE

Nicholas BLAKE
Crime

Margery ALLINGHAM
Simon BRETT
John Dickson CARR
Agatha CHRISTIE
Edmund CRISPIN

James P. BLAYCOCK
Fantasy

August DERLETH
Colin GREENLAND
Robert HOLDSTOCK
H.P. LOVECRAFT
Brian LUMLEY

James BLISH
Science Fiction

Isaac ASIMOV
Ray BRADBURY
Arthur C. CLARKE
John WYNDHAM

Robert BLOCH
Fantasy

Poul ANDERSON
Ray BRADBURY
M. John HARRISON
Robert HOLDSTOCK
H.P. LOVECRAFT

Philip BOAST
Family Stories

Lena KENNEDY

Connie MONK

Catrin MORGAN

E.V. THOMPSON

Dirk BOGARDE
General

Noel BARBER

Elizabeth BOWEN

Robert GODDARD

Larry BOND
Adventure

Robert CARTER

Jack HIGGINS

Michael HARTLAND

Martin BOOTH
Adventure

Robert CARTER

James CLAVELL

Christopher NICOLE

Marc OLDEN

Eric VAN LUSTBADER

Pat BOOTH
The 'Smart Set'

Sandra BROWN

Jackie COLLINS

Judith KRANTZ

Lynda LA PLANTE

Harold ROBBINS

Elizabeth BOWEN
General

Phyllis BENTLEY

Dirk BOGARDE

Anita BROOKNER

Ivy COMPTON-BURNETT

Monica DICKENS

Graham GREENE

Molly KEANE

Rosamond LEHMANN

Olivia MANNING

Iris MURDOCH

Mary WESLEY

Harry BOWLING
Family Stories

Emma BLAIR

Catherine COOKSON

Helen FORRESTER

Lena KENNEDY

Beryl KINGSTON

Hilda McKENZIE

Catherine MARCHANT

Maisie MOSCO

Pamela OLDFIELD

Claire RAYNER

Judith SAXTON

Mary Jane STAPLES

Christine THOMAS

Dee WILLIAMS

Ted WILLIS

William BOYD
General

Kingsley AMIS

Martin AMIS

Julian BARNES

Malcolm BRADBURY

Graham GREENE

Kazuo ISHIGURO

Thomas KENEALLY

Milan KUNDERA

David LODGE

Paul MICOU

Brian MOORE

Caryl PHILLIPS

Paul THEROUX

Clare BOYLAN
Family Stories

Maeve BINCHY

Kathleen CONLON

Edna O'BRIEN

Wendy PERRIAM

Sue TOWNSEND

Malcolm BRADBURY
General

Kingsley AMIS

Martin AMIS

Stan BARSTOW

William BOYD

Melvyn BRAGG

John BRAINE

William COOPER

J.P. DONLEAVY

Michael FRAYN

Martyn HARRIS

Howard JACOBSON

Thomas KENEALLY

David LODGE

John MORTIMER

Tom SHARPE

Alan SILLITOE

David STOREY

Leslie THOMAS

Keith WATERHOUSE

Evelyn WAUGH

A.N. WILSON

Angus WILSON

Ray BRADBURY
Fantasy

Brian W. ALDISS
Poul ANDERSON
J.G. BALLARD
Iain M. BANKS
James BLISH
Robert BLOCH
Terry BROOKS
Harlan ELLISON
David A. GEMMELL
Harry HARRISON
Robert A. HEINLEIN
Frank HERBERT
Ursula LE GUIN
H.P. LOVECRAFT
Richard MATHESON
Frederik POHL
Christopher PRIEST
Tom REAMY
Robert SILVERBERG
Clifford D. SIMAK
Dan SIMMONS
Gene WOLFE
John WYNDHAM
Roger ZELAZNY

Barbara Taylor BRADFORD
Family Stories

Elizabeth ADLER
Jacqueline BRISKIN
Brenda CLARKE
Rosemary ENRIGHT
Cynthia FREEMAN
Susan HOWATCH
Brenda JAGGER
Sheelagh KELLY
Adam KENNEDY
Rosamunde PILCHER
Judith SAXTON
Danielle STEEL
Janet TANNER
Nicola THORNE
Elizabeth VILLARS

Marion Zimmer BRADLEY
Fantasy

Raymond E. FEIST
David A. GEMMELL
Garry D. KILWORTH
Anne McCAFFREY
Melanie RAWN
Tad WILLIAMS

Gillian BRADSHAW
Historical

Dorothy DUNNETT
Robert GRAVES
Barbara HAMLYN
Patrick O'BRIAN

Mary RENAULT

Gore VIDAL

Louis L'AMOUR

Nelson NYE

Melvyn BRAGG
General

Stan BARSTOW

H.E. BATES

Malcolm BRADBURY

Lettice COOPER

Margaret DRABBLE

John FOWLES

D.H. LAWRENCE

Stanley MIDDLETON

John BRAINE
General

Kingsley AMIS

Stan BARSTOW

Malcolm BRADBURY

Alan SILLITOE

Leslie THOMAS

Max BRAND
Western

Al CODY

J.T. EDSON

Zane GREY

Wade HAMILTON

Celia BRAYFIELD
The 'Smart Set'

Jackie COLLINS

Shirley CONRAN

Jilly COOPER

Lynda LA PLANTE

Harold ROBBINS

Thomas TRYON

Penny VINCENZI

Madeleine BRENT
Historical

Dorothy EDEN

Elizabeth HARRIS

Victoria HOLT

Sara HYLTON

Anya SETON

Mary STEWART

Simon BRETT
Crime

Catherine AIRD

Marian BABSON

Robert BARNARD

Nicholas BLAKE

Colin DEXTER

Simon BRETT (cont.)

Elizabeth FERRARS

Jonathan GASH

Tim HEALD

H.R.F. KEATING

Susan MOODY

Michael PEARCE

Mike RIPLEY

Douglas RUTHERFORD

Mark TIMLIN

Colin WATSON

David BRIERLEY
Adventure

Dick FRANCIS

Adam HALL

Helen MACINNES

Freda BRIGHT
The 'Smart Set'

Jacqueline BRISKIN

Julie ELLIS

Judith KRANTZ

June Flaum SINGER

David BRIN
Science Fiction

Brian W. ALDISS

Poul ANDERSON

John BRUNNER

Pat CADIGAN

Philip K. DICK

William GIBSON

Andre BRINK
General

Saul BELLOW

J.M. COETZEE

Buchi EMECHETA

Nadine GORDIMER

Christopher HOPE

Thomas KENEALLY

Alan PATON

Jacqueline BRISKIN
The 'Smart Set'

Celia BRAYFIELD

Freda BRIGHT

Judith KRANTZ

June Flaum SINGER

Barbara TRAPIDO

Iris BROMIGE
Romance

Lucilla ANDREWS

Elizabeth CADELL

Dorothy EDEN

Charlotte LAMB

Mary PEARCE

Rosamunde PILCHER

Susan SALLIS

D.E. STEVENSON

Elswyth THANE

Anita BROOKNER
General

Patricia ANGADI

A.L. BARKER

Elizabeth BOWEN

A.S. BYATT

Margaret DRABBLE

Penelope FITZGERALD

Margaret FORSTER

Penelope LIVELY

Alison LURIE

Barbara PYM

Bernice RUBENS

Gillian TINDALL

William TREVOR

Joanna TROLLOPE

Mary WESLEY

Terry BROOKS
Fantasy

Ray BRADBURY

Stephen DONALDSON

David EDDINGS

Raymond E. FEIST

Terry PRATCHETT

J.R.R. TOLKIEN

Margaret WEIS

Brigid BROPHY
General

Nadine GORDIMER

Iris MURDOCH

Edna O'BRIEN

Muriel SPARK

D.K. BROSTER
Historical

Elizabeth BYRD

Elizabeth CHADWICK

Georgette HEYER

Neil MUNRO

Diana NORMAN

Jean STUBBS

Nigel TRANTER

George Mackay BROWN
General

Robin JENKINS

Richard LLEWELLYN

David NOBBS

Iain Crichton SMITH

Sandra BROWN
The 'Smart Set'

Pat BOOTH

Julie BURCHILL

Elizabeth GAGE

Harold ROBBINS

June Flaum SINGER

Jacqueline SUSANN

John BRUNNER
Science Fiction

David BRIN

Pat CADIGAN

William GIBSON

Bruce STERLING

John BUCHAN
Adventure

Eric AMBLER

Peter DRISCOLL

Ian FLEMING

Robert GODDARD

Jack HIGGINS

Geoffrey HOUSEHOLD

Hammond INNES

Duncan KYLE

Helen MACINNES

Julie BURCHILL
The 'Smart Set'

Sally BEAUMAN

Sandra BROWN

Jackie COLLINS

Joan COLLINS

Elizabeth GAGE

Harold ROBBINS

Pat BURDEN
Crime

Marian BABSON

Elizabeth LEMARCHAND

Anne MORICE

Emma PAGE

Anthony BURGESS
General

Peter ACKROYD

J.G. BALLARD

Saul BELLOW

Robertson DAVIES

Lawrence DURRELL

William GOLDING

Alasdair GRAY

Gabriel Garcia MARQUEZ

George ORWELL

Salman RUSHDIE

Vikram SETH

C.P. SNOW

Paul THEROUX

John UPDIKE

Angus WILSON

Anita BURGH
General

Daphne DU MAURIER

Winston GRAHAM

Maisie MOSCO

James Lee BURKE
Crime

William BAYER

James HALL

Tony HILLERMAN

Tom KAKONIS

Joseph KOENIG

Elmore LEONARD

David L. LINDSEY

Sara PARETSKY

John SANDFORD

W.J. BURLEY
Crime

Catherine AIRD

Douglas CLARK

Nicolas FREELING

Jonathan GASH

B.M. GILL

Martha GRIMES

Roy HART

S.T. HAYMON

Mark HEBDEN

Reginald HILL

Alan HUNTER

H.R.F. KEATING

Roger ORMEROD

John PENN

Sheila RADLEY

Jonathan ROSS

June THOMSON

M.J. TROW

Ted WOOD

Betty BURTON
General

Charlotte Vale ALLEN

Tessa BARCLAY

Virginia COFFMAN

Elizabeth DAISH

Iris GOWER

Claire RAYNER

Gwendoline BUTLER
Crime

Margery ALLINGHAM

Jennie MELVILLE

Gwendoline BUTLER (cont.)

Iain PEARS

Michael UNDERWOOD

A.S. BYATT
General

Peter ACKROYD

Margaret ATWOOD

Anita BROOKNER

Angela CARTER

Margaret DRABBLE

Sally EMERSON

Elizabeth Jane HOWARD

Penelope LIVELY

Candia McWILLIAM

Deborah MOGGACH

Iris MURDOCH

Jane ROGERS

Rose TREMAIN

Marina WARNER

Elizabeth BYRD
Historical

D. K. BROSTER

Elizabeth CHADWICK

Dorothy DUNNETT

Barbara HAMLYN

Neil MUNRO

Anya SETON

Jean STUBBS

Elizabeth CADELL
Romance

Iris BROMIGE

Janet DAILEY

Elvi RHODES

Susan SALLIS

D.E. STEVENSON

Essie SUMMERS

Elswyth THANE

Pat CADIGAN
Science Fiction

David BRIN

John BRUNNER

William GIBSON

K.W. JETER

James M. CAIN
Crime

Raymond CHANDLER

James Hadley CHASE

James ELLROY

Frances FYFIELD

John D. MACDONALD

Mickey SPILLANE

Ross THOMAS

Jim THOMPSON

Andrew VACHSS

Erskine CALDWELL
General

William FAULKNER

Ernest HEMINGWAY

Carson McCULLERS

John STEINBECK

Douglas SCOTT

Antony TREW

John WINGATE

John WINTON

Richard WOODMAN

Taylor CALDWELL
General

Thomas ARMSTRONG

Phyllis BENTLEY

A.J. CRONIN

Daphne DU MAURIER

Howard SPRING

Marguerite STEEN

Brian CALLISON
Sea

Eric J. COLLENETTE

Bernard CORNWELL

Alexander FULLERTON

John HARRIS

Hammond INNES

Geoffrey JENKINS

Alexander KENT

Duncan KYLE

Philip McCUTCHAN

Dudley POPE

Douglas REEMAN

Ramsey CAMPBELL
Supernatural

Steve HARRIS

James HERBERT

Stephen KING

Dean R. KOONTZ

H.P. LOVECRAFT

Graham MASTERTON

Robert CAMPBELL
Crime

James Hadley CHASE

Andrew COBURN

Elmore LEONARD

Rex STOUT

Albert CAMUS
General

Günter GRASS

Herman HESSE

Jack KEROUAC

Ethan CANIN
General

Lisa ALTHER

John COHEN

Laurie COLWIN

Garrison KEILLOR

Sue MILLER

Mary MORRIS

Anne TYLER

Victor CANNING
Adventure

Eric AMBLER

Desmond BAGLEY

Jon CLEARY

Daphne DU MAURIER

Hammond INNES

Robert LUDLUM

Alistair MACLEAN

John MASTERS

Nevil SHUTE

Truman CAPOTE
General

William FAULKNER

Ernest HEMINGWAY

Barry HINES

Carson McCULLERS

Armistead MAUPIN

J.D. SALINGER

Orson Scott CARD
Science Fiction

Arthur C. CLARKE

Alan Dean FOSTER

Stephen KING

Stanislaw LEM

Peter CAREY
General

Peter ACKROYD

John BANVILLE

Rodney HALL

Thomas KENEALLY

David MALOUF

Patrick WHITE

Augustus CARP
Humour

Jerome K. JEROME

A.G. MACDONELL

Barry PAIN

P.G. WODEHOUSE

John Dickson CARR
Crime

Nicholas BLAKE

John Newton CHANCE

Leslie CHARTERIS

John CREASEY

Edmund CRISPIN

Freeman Wills CROFTS

Erle Stanley GARDNER

Michael GILBERT

Michael INNES

H.R.F. KEATING

Ngaio MARSH

Gladys MITCHELL

Dorothy L. SAYERS

Rex STOUT

Julian SYMONS

Josephine TEY

Sara WOODS

Philippa CARR
Historical

Valerie ANAND

Pamela BELLE

Emma DRUMMOND

Dorothy DUNNETT

Valerie GEORGESON

Cynthia HARROD-EAGLES

Isabelle HOLLAND

Victoria HOLT

Brenda JAGGER

Dinah LAMPITT

Claire LORRIMER

Diana NORMAN

Michael CARSON
General

Patrick GALE

Alan HOLLINGHURST

Adam MARS-JONES

Edmund WHITE

Angela CARTER
General

A.S. BYATT

Alice Thomas ELLIS

John FOWLES

Elizabeth JOLLEY

Salman RUSHDIE

Isaac Bashevis SINGER

Fay WELDON

Jeanette WINTERSON

Brian CARTER
General

Aeron CLEMENT

William HORWOOD

A.R. LLOYD

Brian PARVIN

Robert CARTER
Adventure

Larry BOND

Martin BOOTH

James CLAVELL

Robert CARTER (cont.)

Michael HARTLAND

Eric VAN LUSTBADER

Joan SMITH

Michael UNDERWOOD

Sara WOODS

Margaret YORKE

Barbara CARTLAND
Romance

Lucilla ANDREWS

Marion CHESNEY

Caroline COURTNEY

Clare DARCY

Emma DARCY

Penny JORDAN

Denise ROBINS

Sheila WALSH

Joyce CARY
General

Ivy COMPTON-BURNETT

Nadine GORDIMER

Doris LESSING

Marguerite STEEN

Sarah CAUDWELL
Crime

Frances FYFIELD

Ellis PETERS

Annette ROOME

Dorothy SIMPSON

Henry CECIL
Humour

E.F. BENSON

A.G. MACDONELL

John MORTIMER

Auberon WAUGH

Nigel WILLIAMS

P.G. WODEHOUSE

Elizabeth CHADWICK
Historical

D.K. BROSTER

Elizabeth BYRD

Georgette HEYER

Norah LOFTS

Jack L. CHALKER
Science Fiction

Poul ANDERSON

Piers ANTHONY

Philip Jose FARMER

Roger ZELAZNY

John Newton CHANCE
Crime

John Dickson CARR

Raymond CHANDLER

Ed McBAIN

James PATTINSON

Leslie CHARTERIS
Crime

John Dickson CARR

Raymond CHANDLER

Ian FLEMING

John GARDNER

Raymond CHANDLER
Crime

James M. CAIN

John Newton CHANCE

Leslie CHARTERIS

James Hadley CHASE

Robert CRAIS

Lindsey DAVIS

Robert FERRIGNO

Erle Stanley GARDNER

Dashiell HAMMETT

Michael INNES

H.R.F. KEATING

John D. MACDONALD

Sara PARETSKY

Robert B. PARKER

Georges SIMENON

Mickey SPILLANE

Rex STOUT

James Hadley CHASE
Crime

James M. CAIN

Robert CAMPBELL

Raymond CHANDLER

K.C. CONSTANTINE

Robert GOLDSBOROUGH

Dashiell HAMMETT

Ed McBAIN

John D. MACDONALD

Robert B. PARKER

Mickey SPILLANE

Rex STOUT

Bruce CHATWIN
General

Julian BARNES

David COOK

John FOWLES

Patrick McCABE

Barry UNSWORTH

Amit CHAUDHURI
General

John MASTERS

Gita MEHTA

R.K. NARAYAN

Vikram SETH

John CHEEVER
General

L.P. HARTLEY

William KENNEDY

John O'HARA

John UPDIKE

Gore VIDAL

C.J. CHERRYH
Science Fiction

Greg BEAR

James P. HOGAN

Anne McCAFFREY

Frederik POHL

Bob SHAW

Marion CHESNEY
Romance

Lucilla ANDREWS

Barbara CARTLAND

Caroline COURTNEY

Clare DARCY

Georgette HEYER

Denise ROBINS

Patricia ROBINS

Sheila WALSH

Matt CHISHOLM
Western

J.T. EDSON

Wade HAMILTON

Louis L'AMOUR

Bill WADE

Agatha CHRISTIE
Crime

Catherine AIRD

Marian BABSON

Josephine BELL

John CREASEY

Edmund CRISPIN

Freeman Wills CROFTS

Elizabeth FERRARS

Antonia FRASER

Elizabeth GEORGE

Michael GILBERT

Ann GRANGER

Martha GRIMES

Emma LATHEN

Elizabeth LEMARCHAND

Ngaio MARSH

Gladys MITCHELL

Dorothy L. SAYERS

Georges SIMENON

Dorothy SIMPSON

Julian SYMONS

Josephine TEY

June THOMSON

Patricia WENTWORTH

Tom CLANCY
Adventure

Ted ALLBEURY

Stephen COONTS

Clive CUSSLER

Nelson DE MILLE

Daniel EASTERMAN

Colin FORBES

Palma HARCOURT

John HARRIS

Jack HIGGINS

Robert LUDLUM

Gerald SEYMOUR

Douglas TERMAN

Craig THOMAS

Douglas CLARK
Crime

W.J. BURLEY

Colin DEXTER

Arthur DOUGLAS

Dick FRANCIS

Roy HART

John SHERWOOD

June THOMSON

Mary Higgins CLARK
Crime

Joy FIELDING

Frances HEGARTY

Jonathan KELLERMAN

Judith KELMAN

Barbara MICHAELS

Anita SHREVE

David WILTSE

Arthur C. CLARKE
Science Fiction

Isaac ASIMOV

Greg BEAR

James BLISH

Orson Scott CARD

Richard COWPER

Robert A. HEINLEIN

Ursula LE GUIN

Stanislaw LEM

Vonda N. MACINTYRE

Larry NIVEN

Frederik POHL

Eric Frank RUSSELL

Bob SHAW

Brenda CLARKE
Family Stories

Barbara Taylor BRADFORD

Brenda JAGGER

Beryl KINGSTON

Miss READ

Kay STEPHENS

Roy CLARKE
Humour

David NOBBS

Tom SHARPE

Peter TINNISWOOD

Sue TOWNSEND

James CLAVELL
Adventure

Martin BOOTH

Robert CARTER

Nelson DE MILLE

Robert ELEGANT

Frederick FORSYTH

Gary JENNINGS

Arthur HAILEY

Michael HARTLAND

John MASTERS

James A. MICHENER

Christopher NICOLE

Alan SAVAGE

Wilbur SMITH

Eric VAN LUSTBADER

Jon CLEARY
Adventure

Desmond BAGLEY

Noel BARBER

Victor CANNING

Francis CLIFFORD

Richard CONDON

Colin FORBES

Brian FREEMANTLE

Alexander FULLERTON

John HARRIS

Hammond INNES

Geoffrey JENKINS

Duncan KYLE

Derek LAMBERT

Gavin LYALL

Alistair MACLEAN

John MASTERS

Harry PATTERSON

Kenneth ROYCE

Douglas RUTHERFORD

Irwin SHAW

Nevil SHUTE

Wilbur SMITH

Morris WEST

Aeron CLEMENT
General

Richard ADAMS

Brian CARTER

William HORWOOD

Brian PARVIN

Carol CLEWLOW
General

Wendy PERRIAM

Daoma WINSTON

Jeanette WINTERSON

Francis CLIFFORD
Adventure

Jon CLEARY

Ian FLEMING

James LEASOR

John LE CARRÉ

Robert LUDLUM

Michael CLYNES
Crime

Ellis PETERS

William KIENZLE

Andrew COBURN
General

Robert CAMPBELL

K.C. CONSTANTINE

Robert CRAIS

Stuart M. KAMINSKY

Robert B. PARKER

Ian COCHRANE
General

James HAMILTON-PATERSON

Ian McEWAN

Al CODY
Western

Max BRAND

J.T. EDSON

Zane GREY

Louis L'AMOUR

Jess CODY
Western

Louis L'AMOUR

J.T. EDSON

Chuck MARTIN

T.C. OLSEN

Liza CODY
Crime

Linda BARNES

Sue GRAFTON

Susan MOODY

Sara PARETSKY

Robert B. PARKER

Ruth RENDELL

J.M. COETZEE
General

Chinua ACHEBE

Andre BRINK

Nadine GORDIMER

Amanda PRANTERA

Barry UNSWORTH

Virginia COFFMAN
Family Stories

Virginia ANDREWS

Betty BURTON

Janet DAILEY

Barbara MICHAELS

Belva PLAIN

Mary STEWART

Jessica STIRLING

Helen VAN SLYKE

Phyllis A. WHITNEY

Daoma WINSTON

Anthea COHEN
Crime

Antonia FRASER

B.M. GILL

Lesley GRANT-ADAMSON

Patricia HIGHSMITH

Simon SHAW

Jon COHEN
General

Ethan CANIN

Sue MILLER

Mary MORRIS

Isabel COLEGATE
General

Penelope FITZGERALD

Georgina HAMMICK

Muriel SPARK

Joanna TROLLOPE

Vernon COLEMAN
General

Frank G. SLAUGHTER

Denys VAL BAKER

Eric J. COLLENETTE
Sea

Brian CALLISON

Douglas SCOTT

Peter TONKIN

Jackie COLLINS
The 'Smart Set'

Sally BEAUMAN

Pat BOOTH

Celia BRAYFIELD

Jacqueline BRISKIN

Julie BURCHILL

Joan COLLINS

Shirley CONRAN

Jilly COOPER

Elizabeth GAGE

Judith GOULD

Judith KRANTZ

Lynda LA PLANTE

Molly PARKIN

Harold ROBBINS

Penny VINCENZI

Joan COLLINS
The 'Smart Set'

Julie BURCHELL

Jackie COLLINS

Elizabeth GAGE

Harold ROBBINS

Nancy COLLINS
Supernatural

Anne RICE

George R. MARTIN

Dan SIMMONS

Norman COLLINS
General

A.J. CRONIN

R.F. DELDERFIELD

J.B. PRIESTLEY

Laurie COLWIN
General

Ethan CANIN

Sue MILLER

Ivy COMPTON-BURNETT
General

Elizabeth BOWEN

Joyce CARY

Marguerite STEEN

Barbara COMYNS
General

Margaret ATWOOD

Janice ELLIOTT

Georgina HAMMICK

Barbara COMYNS (cont.)

Muriel SPARK

Joanna TROLLOPE

Henry JAMES

W. Somerset MAUGHAM

Patrick O'BRIAN

Richard CONDON
Adventure

Simon BELL

Jon CLEARY

Richard COX

Michael CRICHTON

Arthur HAILEY

John LE CARRÉ

Thomas PERRY

Sidney SHELDON

Leslie WALLER

Donald WESTLAKE

Kathleen CONLON
Family Stories

Maeve BINCHY

Clare BOYLAN

Frank DELANEY

Elizabeth Jane HOWARD

Molly KEANE

Joseph CONRAD
General

Graham GREENE

Ernest HEMINGWAY

Shirley CONRAN
The 'Smart Set'

Celia BRAYFIELD

Jackie COLLINS

Jilly COOPER

Harold ROBBINS

Thomas TRYON

Penny VINCENZI

K.C. CONSTANTINE
Crime

James Hadley CHASE

Andrew COBURN

Ed McBAIN

David COOK
General

Paul BAILEY

Bruce CHATWIN

Ian McEWAN

Stanley MIDDLETON

Brian MOORE

Paul SAYER

Hugh COOK
Fantasy

Michael MOORCOCK

J.R.R. TOLKIEN

Robin COOK
Adventure

Simon BELL

Lawrence SANDERS

Frank G. SLAUGHTER

Catherine COOKSON
Family Stories

Tessa BARCLAY

Emma BLAIR

Harry BOWLING

Josephine COX

Mazo DE LA ROCHE

Dorothy EDEN

Cynthia FREEMAN

Catherine GAVIN

Iris GOWER

Margaret GRAHAM

Audrey HOWARD

Brenda JAGGER

Marie JOSEPH

Lena KENNEDY

Claire LORRIMER

Catherine MARCHANT

Mary E. PEARCE

Elvi RHODES

D.E. STEVENSON

Jean STUBBS

Janet TANNER

Grace THOMPSON

Stephen COONTS
Adventure

Tom CLANCY

Jilly COOPER
The 'Smart Set'

Sally BEAUMAN

Celia BRAYFIELD

Jackie COLLINS

Shirley CONRAN

Elizabeth GAGE

Judith GOULD

Judith KRANTZ

Harold ROBBINS

June Flaum SINGER

Barbara TRAPIDO

Lettice COOPER
General

Melvyn BRAGG

Winifred HOLTBY

Mervyn JONES

Angela THIRKELL

William COOPER
General

Kingsley AMIS

Malcolm BRADBURY

Stanley MIDDLETON

C.P. SNOW

J.I.M. STEWART

Alexander CORDELL
General

A.J. CRONIN

Iris GOWER

Winston GRAHAM

Richard LLEWELLYN

Malcolm MACDONALD

Howard SPRING

E.V. THOMPSON

Barry CORK
Crime

Dick FRANCIS

John FRANCOME

Bernard CORNWELL
Adventure

Brian CALLISON

Alan EVANS

C.S. FORESTER

Alexander FULLERTON

Max HENNESSY

Alexander KENT

Sam LLEWELLYN

Patrick O'BRIAN

Douglas REEMAN

Nigel TRANTER

Richard WOODMAN

Patricia D. CORNWELL
Crime

Frances FYFIELD

Sue GRAFTON

John GRISHAM

Jonathan KELLERMAN

Ruth RENDELL

William J. COUGHLIN
Crime

Philip FRIEDMAN

John GRISHAM

Caroline COURTNEY
Romance

Barbara CARTLAND

Marion CHESNEY

Clare DARCY

Richard COWPER
Science Fiction

Brian W. ALDISS
Arthur C. CLARKE
Vonda N. MACINTYRE
Clifford D. SIMAK
Brian STABLEFORD

Josephine COX
General

Charlotte Vale ALLEN
Catherine COOKSON
Iris GOWER
Marie JOSEPH
Lena KENNEDY
Beryl KINGSTON
Catherine MARCHANT
Maisie MOSCO
Susan SALLIS
Sarah SHEARS

Richard COX
Adventure

Richard CONDON
Arthur HAILEY
Thomas PERRY
Leslie WALLER

Robert CRAIS
Crime

Raymond CHANDLER
Andrew COBURN
James HALL
Elmore LEONARD

Teresa CRANE
Historical

Catherine GASKIN
Genevieve LYONS
Belva PLAIN
Judith SAXTON

John CREASEY
Crime

John Dickson CARR
Agatha CHRISTIE
Dick FRANCIS
John Buxton HILTON
Ed McBAIN
Jonathan ROSS
Georges SIMENON

Michael CRICHTON
General

Simon BELL
Richard CONDON

Michael CRICHTON (cont.)

John GRISHAM

Mario PUZO

Gladys MITCHELL

Rex STOUT

Josephine TEY

Edmund CRISPIN
Crime

Margery ALLINGHAM

Nicholas BLAKE

John Dickson CARR

Agatha CHRISTIE

Michael INNES

Ngaio MARSH

Gladys MITCHELL

Josephine TEY

Colin WATSON

Julian CRITCHLEY
General

Susan CROSLAND

Michael DOBBS

Bertie DENHAM

Freeman Wills CROFTS
Crime

Margery ALLINGHAM

John Dickson CARR

Agatha CHRISTIE

A.J. CRONIN
General

Thomas ARMSTRONG

H.E. BATES

Phyllis BENTLEY

Taylor CALDWELL

Norman COLLINS

Alexander CORDELL

R.F. DELDERFIELD

Henry DENKER

Winston GRAHAM

Graham GREENE

Richard LLEWELLYN

J.B. PRIESTLEY

Frank G. SLAUGHTER

Howard SPRING

Susan CROSLAND
General

Julian CRITCHLEY

Bertie DENHAM

Michael DOBBS

Amanda CROSS
Crime

Linda BARNES

Antonia FRASER

Elizabeth GEORGE

Sue GRAFTON

Emma LATHEN

Ursula CURTISS
Romance

Phyllis A. WHITNEY

Margaret YORKE

Clive CUSSLER
Adventure

Desmond BAGLEY

Tom CLANCY

Len DEIGHTON

Alan EVANS

Frederick FORSYTH

Hammond INNES

Alistair MACLEAN

Douglas REEMAN

Gerald SEYMOUR

Craig THOMAS

Janet DAILEY
Family Stories

Charlotte Vale ALLEN

Elizabeth CADELL

Virginia COFFMAN

John Gordon DAVIS

Charlotte LAMB

Anne MATHER

Pamela OLDFIELD

Belva PLAIN

Judith SAXTON

Diana STAINFORTH

Danielle STEEL

Margaret SUNLEY

Janet TANNER

Helen VAN SLYKE

Daoma WINSTON

Elizabeth DAISH
Family Stories

Tessa BARCLAY

Betty BURTON

Mark DANIEL
Crime

Arthur DOUGLAS

Dick FRANCIS

John FRANCOME

Douglas RUTHERFORD

Clare DARCY
Romance

Barbara CARTLAND

Marion CHESNEY

Caroline COURTNEY

Emma DARCY
Romance

Barbara CARTLAND

Doris DAVIDSON
Family Stories

Margaret Thomson DAVIS

Jessica STIRLING

Robertson DAVIES
General

Kingsley AMIS

H.E. BATES

Anthony BURGESS

John Gordon DAVIS
Family Stories

Janet DAILEY

Colleen McCULLOUGH

Una-Mary PARKER

Eileen TOWNSEND

Lindsey DAVIS
Crime

Raymond CHANDLER

P.C. DOHERTY

Elizabeth EYRE

John Buxton HILTON

Ellis PETERS

Margaret Thomson DAVIS
Family Stories

Tessa BARCLAY

Emma BLAIR

Doris DAVIDSON

Christine Marion FRASER

Iris GOWER

Evelyn HOOD

Marie JOSEPH

Lena KENNEDY

Jessica STIRLING

Reay TANNAHILL

Nicola THORNE

Len DEIGHTON
Adventure

Clive CUSSLER

Nelson DE MILLE

Clive EGLETON

Ian FLEMING

Ken FOLLETT

Colin FORBES

Frederick FORSYTH

Brian FREEMANTLE

John GARDNER

Adam HALL

Philip KERR

Derek LAMBERT

John LE CARRÉ

Gavin LYALL

Harry PATTERSON

Anthony PRICE

Kenneth ROYCE

Tim SEBASTIAN

Gerald SEYMOUR

Frank DELANEY
Family Stories

Maeve BINCHY

Kathleen CONLON

Audrey HOWARD

Deirdre PURCELL

Jamie DELANO
Fantasy

Clive BARKER

Neil GAIMAN

Dave GIBBONS

Frank MILLER

Alan MOORE

John WAGNER

Samuel R. DELANY
Science Fiction

Harlan ELLISON

Michael MOORCOCK

Joanna RUSS

Roger ZELAZNY

Mazo DE LA ROCHE
Family Stories

Thomas ARMSTRONG

Catherine COOKSON

R.F. DELDERFIELD

Elizabeth GOUDGE

Winston GRAHAM

Winifred HOLTBY

Rosalind LAKER

Claire RAYNER

D.E. STEVENSON

Jessica STIRLING

R.F. DELDERFIELD
Family Stories

Thomas ARMSTRONG

Noel BARBER

H.E. BATES

Phyllis BENTLEY

Norman COLLINS

A.J. CRONIN

Mazo DE LA ROCHE

Rumer GODDEN

R.F. DELDERFIELD (cont.)

Iris GOWER
Winston GRAHAM
Sarah HARRISON
Elizabeth Jane HOWARD
Susan HOWATCH
Anne MELVILLE
J.B. PRIESTLEY
Howard SPRING
E.V. THOMPSON
Eileen TOWNSEND

Nelson DE MILLE
Adventure

Desmond BAGLEY
Tom CLANCY
James CLAVELL
Len DEIGHTON
Daniel EASTERMAN
Colin FORBES
Jack HIGGINS
Gary JENNINGS
James A. MICHENER
Sidney SHELDON
Craig THOMAS
John TRENHAILE

Bertie DENHAM
General

Julian CRITCHLEY
Susan CROSLAND
Michael DOBBS

Henry DENKER
General

A.J. CRONIN
Arthur HAILEY
Frank G. SLAUGHTER

August DERLETH
Fantasy

James P. BLAYCOCK
Robert HOLDSTOCK
H.P. LOVECRAFT
Clark Ashton SMITH

Anita DESAI
General

Margaret ATWOOD
Ruth Prawer JHABVALA
Russell LUCAS
Iris MURDOCH
R.K. NARAYAN

Colin DEXTER
Crime

Robert BARNARD

Simon BRETT

Douglas CLARK

Nicolas FREELING

Jonathan GASH

Elizabeth GEORGE

John HARVEY

Reginald HILL

Michael INNES

P.D. JAMES

Peter LOVESEY

Roger ORMEROD

Ruth RENDELL

R.D. WINGFIELD

Eric WRIGHT

Michael DIBDIN
Crime

Peter DICKINSON

P.D. JAMES

Elmore LEONARD

James McCLURE

Magdalen NABB

Philip K. DICK
Science Fiction

Isaac ASIMOV

J.G. BALLARD

David BRIN

William GIBSON

Robert A. HEINLEIN

K.W. JETER

Rudy RUCKER

Ian WATSON

Monica DICKENS
Family Stories

Lynne Reid BANKS

H.E. BATES

Nina BAWDEN

Elizabeth BOWEN

Dorothy EDEN

Janice ELLIOTT

Margaret FORSTER

Paul GALLICO

Rumer GODDEN

Elizabeth Jane HOWARD

Penelope LIVELY

Norah LOFTS

Joy PACKER

Mary E. PEARCE

Barbara PYM

Miss READ

Margery SHARP

Howard SPRING

D.E. STEVENSON

Elizabeth TAYLOR

Peter DICKINSON
Crime

Michael DIBDIN

P.D. JAMES

Gordon R. DICKSON
Science Fiction

Poul ANDERSON

Robert SILVERBERG

Clifford D. SIMAK

Roger ZELAZNY

Joyce DINGWELL
Romance

Charlotte LAMB

Anne MATHER

Carole MORTIMER

Jessica STEELE

Jenny DISKI
General

Beryl BAINBRIDGE

Joyce Carol OATES

Michael DOBBS
General

Jeffrey ARCHER

Julian CRITCHLEY

Susan CROSLAND

Bertie DENHAM

Tom HOLT

David LODGE

Keith WATERHOUSE

E.L. DOCTOROW
General

F. Scott FITZGERALD

Thomas KENEALLY

William KENNEDY

Toni MORRISON

Jane SMILEY

John UPDIKE

P.C. DOHERTY
Crime

Lindsey DAVIS

D.M. GREENWOOD

Ellis PETERS

Anabel DONALD
General

Anne FINE

Deborah MOGGACH

Bel MOONEY

Stephen DONALDSON
Fantasy

Jean M. AUEL

Terry BROOKS

David EDDINGS

Stephen KING

J.R.R. TOLKIEN

J.P. DONLEAVY
General

Malcolm BRADBURY

Flann O'BRIEN

Tom SHARPE

Jane DONNELLY
Romance

Charlotte LAMB

Anne MATHER

Carole MORTIMER

Jessica STEELE

Arthur DOUGLAS
Crime

Douglas CLARK

Mark DANIEL

Dick FRANCIS

Colin DOUGLAS
Humour

Richard GORDON

David NOBBS

Ellen DOUGLAS
General

Ellen GILCHRIST

Gloria NAYLOR

Alice WALKER

Roddy DOYLE
Humour

Martin AMIS

Guy BELLAMY

Geoff DYER

James KELMAN

David NOBBS

Nicholas SALAMAN

Margaret DRABBLE
General

Joan AIKEN

Beryl BAINBRIDGE

Lynne Reid BANKS

Nina BAWDEN

Melvyn BRAGG

Margaret DRABBLE (cont.)

Anita BROOKNER
A.S. BYATT
Daphne DU MAURIER
Alice Thomas ELLIS
Penelope FITZGERALD
Margaret FORSTER
Marilyn FRENCH
Susan HILL
Elizabeth Jane HOWARD
Penelope LIVELY
Alison LURIE
Olivia MANNING
Penelope MORTIMER
Iris MURDOCH
Edna O'BRIEN
Barbara PYM
Jean RHYS
Bernice RUBENS
Margery SHARP
Muriel SPARK
Elizabeth TAYLOR
Gillian TINDALL
Joanna TROLLOPE
Fay WELDON

Peter DRISCOLL
Adventure

Eric AMBLER
John BUCHAN
Nicholas GUILD

Emma DRUMMOND
Historical

Pamela BELLE
Philippa CARR
Cynthia HARROD-EAGLES
Victoria HOLT

Daphne DU MAURIER
General

Anita BURGH
Taylor CALDWELL
Victor CANNING
Margaret DRABBLE
Margaret FORSTER
Catherine GAVIN
Robert GODDARD
Winston GRAHAM
Susan HILL
Jane Aiken HODGE
Winifred HOLTBY
Susan HOWATCH
Norah LOFTS
Barbara MICHAELS
Joy PACKER
Anya SETON
Mary STEWART
E.V. THOMPSON
Joanna TROLLOPE
Denys VAL BAKER
Mary WESLEY

Jane DUNCAN
Family Stories

Miss READ

Sarah SHEARS

D.E. STEVENSON

Dorothy DUNNETT
Historical

Valerie ANAND

Evelyn ANTHONY

Pamela BELLE

Gillian BRADSHAW

Elizabeth BYRD

Philippa CARR

Winston GRAHAM

Georgette HEYER

Diana NORMAN

Edith PARGETER

Jean PLAIDY

Mary RENAULT

Anya SETON

Mary STEWART

Reay TANNAHILL

Nigel TRANTER

Lawrence DURRELL
General

Kingsley AMIS

Anthony BURGESS

Graham GREENE

Olivia MANNING

C.P. SNOW

John UPDIKE

Geoff DYER
General

Roddy DOYLE

J.D. SALINGER

Daniel EASTERMAN
Adventure

Tom CLANCY

Nelson DE MILLE

James FOLLETT

John TRENHAILE

David EDDINGS
Fantasy

Robert ADAMS

Terry BROOKS

Stephen DONALDSON

Raymond E. FEIST

David A. GEMMELL

Robert JORDAN

Guy Gavriel KAY

Katherine KERR

Garry D. KILWORTH

Anne McCAFFREY

Melanie RAWN

David EDDINGS (cont.)

J.R.R. TOLKIEN

Margaret WEIS

Tad WILLIAMS

Dorothy EDEN
General

Phyllis BENTLEY

Madeleine BRENT

Iris BROMIGE

Catherine COOKSON

Monica DICKENS

Barbara MICHAELS

Anya SETON

Marguerite STEEN

Anne STEVENSON

Mary STEWART

Phyllis A. WHITNEY

J.T. EDSON
Western

Max BRAND

Matt CHISHOLM

Al CODY

Jess CODY

Louis L'AMOUR

Nelson NYE

Lesley EGAN
Crime

Eugene IZZI

Ed McBAIN

Dell SHANNON

Clive EGLETON
Adventure

Ted ALLBEURY

Len DEIGHTON

Colin FORBES

Frederick FORSYTH

Palma HARCOURT

John KATZENBACH

John LE CARRÉ

Robert LUDLUM

Alistair MACLEAN

Anthony PRICE

Sidney SHELDON

Robert ELEGANT
General

James CLAVELL

James A. MICHENER

Alan SAVAGE

Eric VAN LUSTBADER

Janice ELLIOTT
General

Margaret ATWOOD
Pat BARKER
Barbara COMYNS
Monica DICKENS
Iris MURDOCH

Alice Thomas ELLIS
General

Hilary BAILEY
Beryl BAINBRIDGE
Angela CARTER
Margaret DRABBLE
Jennifer JOHNSTON
Molly KEANE
Penelope LIVELY
Deborah MOGGACH
Edna O'BRIEN
Barbara PYM
Bernice RUBENS
Muriel SPARK

Julie ELLIS
The 'Smart Set'

Freda BRIGHT
Sarah HARRISON
Lynda LA PLANTE
June Flaum SINGER

Harlan ELLISON
Science Fiction

Poul ANDERSON
Ray BRADBURY
Samuel R. DELANY

Ralph ELLISON
General

Toni MORRISON
William STYRON
Richard WRIGHT

James ELLROY
Crime

James M. CAIN
Dashiell HAMMETT
Elmore LEONARD
Walter MOSLEY
Jim THOMPSON

Ben ELTON
General

Douglas ADAMS
Kingsley AMIS
Martyn HARRIS
Carl HIAASEN
Michael MALONE

Buchi EMECHETA
General

Andre BRINK

Nadine GORDIMER

Toni MORRISON

Sally EMERSON
General

A.S. BYATT

Janice GALLOWAY

Candia McWILLIAM

Jane ROGERS

Shusako ENDO
General

Russell BANKS

Kazuo ISHIGURO

Yukio MISHIMA

Rosemary ENRIGHT
Family Stories

Tessa BARCLAY

Barbara Taylor BRADFORD

Maisie MOSCO

Pamela OLDFIELD

Louise ERDRICH
General

William FAULKNER

Alison LURIE

Lorrie MOORE

Anne TYLER

Barbara ERSKINE
Historical

Evelyn ANTHONY

Cynthia HARROD-EAGLES

Margaret ERSKINE
Family Stories

Catherine GASKIN

Judith GLOVER

Gavin ESLER
Adventure

Ian ST. JAMES

Tim SEBASTIAN

Gerald SEYMOUR

Loren D. ESTLEMAN
Crime

William BAYER

Dashiell HAMMETT

Elmore LEONARD

Alan EVANS
Adventure

Ronald BASSETT

Bernard CORNWELL

Clive CUSSLER

Max HENNESSY

Douglas SCOTT

Peter TONKIN

Elizabeth EYRE
Crime

Lindsey DAVIS

Ellis PETERS

Zoe FAIRBAIRNS
Family Stories

Kate FLYNN

Susan HOWATCH

Reay TANNAHILL

Philip Jose FARMER
Science Fiction

Piers ANTHONY

Greg BEAR

Jack L. CHALKER

J.G. FARRELL
General

Peter ACKROYD

Christopher HUDSON

Ruth Prawer JHABVALA

John MASTERS

Flann O'BRIEN

John FARRIS
Supernatural

Stephen KING

Dean R. KOONTZ

Robert McCAMMON

Howard FAST
General

Saul BELLOW

Winston GRAHAM

Leon URIS

Herman WOUK

William FAULKNER
General

Saul BELLOW

Truman CAPOTE

Erskine CALDWELL

Louise ERDRICH

F. Scott FITZGERALD

Ellen GILCHRIST

Ernest HEMINGWAY

William FAULKNER (cont.)

Bobbie Ann MASON

John STEINBECK

William STYRON

Peter TAYLOR

Sebastian FAULKS
General

Julian BARNES

Ronald FRAME

Milan KUNDERA

Raymond E. FEIST
Fantasy

Marion Zimmer BRADLEY

Terry BROOKS

David EDDINGS

Robert JORDAN

Anne McCAFFREY

Andre NORTON

Margaret WEIS

Elizabeth FERRARS
Crime

Catherine AIRD

Marian BABSON

Simon BRETT

Agatha CHRISTIE

Antonia FRASER

Martha GRIMES

Emma LATHEN

Ngaio MARSH

Roger ORMEROD

John PENN

Dorothy SIMPSON

June THOMSON

Margaret YORKE

Robert FERRIGNO
Crime

Raymond CHANDLER

Mickey SPILLANE

Joy FIELDING
Crime

Mary Higgins CLARK

Jonathan KELLERMAN

Judith KELMAN

Anne FINE
General

Anabel DONALD

Deborah MOGGACH

Bel MOONEY

F. Scott FITZGERALD
General

E.L. DOCTOROW

William FAULKNER

Ford Maddox FORD

E.M. FORSTER

John GALSWORTHY

Graham GREENE

L.P. HARTLEY

Henry JAMES

Sinclair LEWIS

Carson McCULLERS

John O'HARA

Anthony POWELL

John STEINBECK

Evelyn WAUGH

Penelope FITZGERALD
General

Beryl BAINBRIDGE

Anita BROOKNER

Isabel COLEGATE

Margaret DRABBLE

Margaret FORSTER

Penelope LIVELY

Iris MURDOCH

Emma TENNANT

Ian FLEMING
Adventure

Eric AMBLER

John BUCHAN

Leslie CHARTERIS

Francis CLIFFORD

Len DEIGHTON

Ken FOLLETT

Brian FREEMANTLE

John GARDNER

Adam HALL

Philip KERR

Robert LUDLUM

Gavin LYALL

Harry PATTERSON

Joe POYER

Kate FLYNN
Family Stories

Lyn ANDREWS

Zoe FAIRBAIRNS

Helen FORRESTER

Audrey HOWARD

Elizabeth MURPHY

James FOLLETT
Adventure

Daniel EASTERMAN

Colin FORBES

Clare FRANCIS

James FOLLETT (cont.)

John HARRIS

Robert LUDLUM

Alistair MACLEAN

Craig THOMAS

John TRENHAILE

Ken FOLLETT
Adventure

Ted ALLBEURY

Jeffrey ARCHER

Desmond BAGLEY

Len DEIGHTON

Ian FLEMING

Colin FORBES

Frederick FORSYTH

Clare FRANCIS

Arthur HAILEY

Palma HARCOURT

Jack HIGGINS

Hammond INNES

John LE CARRÉ

Robert LUDLUM

Alistair MACLEAN

Lawrence SANDERS

Wilbur SMITH

Craig THOMAS

Colin FORBES
Adventure

Ted ALLBEURY

Evelyn ANTHONY

Campbell ARMSTRONG

Tom CLANCY

Jon CLEARY

Nelson DE MILLE

Len DEIGHTON

Clive EGLETON

James FOLLETT

Ken FOLLETT

Frederick FORSYTH

Palma HARCOURT

Jack HIGGINS

Geoffrey JENKINS

John LE CARRÉ

Helen MACINNES

Anthony PRICE

Gerald SEYMOUR

Craig THOMAS

John TRENHAILE

Ford Maddox FORD
General

F. Scott FITZGERALD

Sinclair LEWIS

John O'HARA

Richard FORD
General

William STYRON

Anne TYLER

John UPDIKE

C.S. FORESTER
Sea

Bernard CORNWELL

Raymond HARDIE

Hammond INNES

Alexander KENT

A.E. LANGSFORD

Nicholas MONSARRAT

Patrick O'BRIAN

Dudley POPE

Douglas REEMAN

Showell STYLES

Victor SUTHREN

John WINTON

Richard WOODMAN

Helen FORRESTER
Family Stories

Lyn ANDREWS

Emma BLAIR

Harry BOWLING

Kate FLYNN

Audrey HOWARD

Marie JOSEPH

Lena KENNEDY

Beryl KINGSTON

Elizabeth MURPHY

Pamela OLDFIELD

Claire RAYNER

Elvi RHODES

Judith SAXTON

Sarah SHEARS

Larry FORRESTER
War

W.E.B. GRIFFIN

Max HENNESSY

Derek ROBINSON

E.M. FORSTER
General

Saul BELLOW

F. Scott FITZGERALD

Graham GREENE

Henry JAMES

Ruth Prawer JHABVALA

D.H. LAWRENCE

John MASTERS

C.P. SNOW

Howard SPRING

Margaret FORSTER
General

Beryl BAINBRIDGE

Nina BAWDEN

Anita BROOKNER

Monica DICKENS

Margaret DRABBLE

Daphne DU MAURIER

Penelope FITZGERALD

Susan HILL

Elizabeth Jane HOWARD

Penelope LIVELY

Alison LURIE

Olivia MANNING

Deborah MOGGACH

Bel MOONEY

Iris MURDOCH

Muriel SPARK

Joanna TROLLOPE

Fay WELDON

Frederick FORSYTH
Adventure

Ted ALLBEURY

James CLAVELL

Clive CUSSLER

Len DEIGHTON

Clive EGLETON

Ken FOLLETT

Colin FORBES

Brian FREEMANTLE

Arthur HAILEY

Jack HIGGINS

Geoffrey JENKINS

Duncan KYLE

Derek LAMBERT

John LE CARRÉ

Gavin LYALL

David MASON

Harry PATTERSON

Gerald SEYMOUR

Craig THOMAS

John TRENHAILE

Elleston TREVOR

Morris WEST

Alan Dean FOSTER
Science Fiction

Piers ANTHONY

Orson Scott CARD

Terry PRATCHETT

Christopher FOWLER
Fantasy

Stephen KING

Graham MASTERTON

John FOWLES
General

Peter ACKROYD
Saul BELLOW
Melvyn BRAGG
Angela CARTER
Bruce CHATWIN
William GOLDING
Stephen GREGORY
Christopher HOPE
D.H. LAWRENCE
Iris MURDOCH
Robert NYE
Salman RUSHDIE
Graham SWIFT
D.M. THOMAS
Barry UNSWORTH

Ronald FRAME
General

Sebastian FAULKS
Kazuo ISHIGURO
Paul MICOU

Clare FRANCIS
Adventure

Evelyn ANTHONY
Desmond BAGLEY
James FOLLETT
Ken FOLLETT
Jack HIGGINS
Geoffrey JENKINS
Duncan KYLE
Helen MACINNES
Mary STEWART

Dick FRANCIS
Crime

David BRIERLEY
Douglas CLARK
Barry CORK
John CREASEY
Mark DANIEL
Arthur DOUGLAS
John FRANCOME
Nicolas FREELING
Michael GELLER
Michael INNES
Richard LONGRIGG
Paul MYERS
Richard PITMAN
Martin RUSSELL
Richard RUSSELL
Douglas RUTHERFORD

John FRANCOME
Crime

Barry CORK
Mark DANIEL
Dick FRANCIS

John FRANCOME (cont.)

Michael GELLER

Richard PITMAN

Douglas RUTHERFORD

Frances PAIGE

Claire RAYNER

Elvi RHODES

Sarah SHEARS

Jessica STIRLING

Jan WEBSTER

Antonia FRASER
Crime

Agatha CHRISTIE

Anthea COHEN

Amanda CROSS

Elizabeth FERRARS

Elizabeth GEORGE

Sue GRAFTON

Lesley GRANT-ADAMSON

Martha GRIMES

Jennie MELVILLE

Anne MORICE

Sara PARETSKY

STAYNES & STOREY

Margaret YORKE

Christine Marion FRASER
Family Stories

Emma BLAIR

Margaret Thomson DAVIS

Valerie GEORGESON

Evelyn HOOD

Susan HOWATCH

Brenda JAGGER

Anne MELVILLE

George Macdonald FRASER
Humour

H.E. BATES

Tom SHARPE

Leslie THOMAS

Peter TINNISWOOD

Gordon WILLIAMS

Sara FRASER
Family Stories

Lyn ANDREWS

Marie JOSEPH

Sarah SHEARS

Janet TANNER

Michael FRAYN
Humour

Douglas ADAMS

Kingsley AMIS

Guy BELLAMY

Malcolm BRADBURY

David NOBBS

Nicolas FREELING
Crime

W.J. BURLEY

Colin DEXTER

Dick FRANCIS

Mark HEBDEN

H.R.F. KEATING

Philip KERR

Ed McBAIN

Georges SIMENON

John LE CARRÉ

Gavin LYALL

Helen MACINNES

Celia FREMLIN
Crime

B.M. GILL

Gerald HAMMOND

Margaret YORKE

Cynthia FREEMAN
Family Stories

Charlotte Vale ALLEN

Emma BLAIR

Barbara Taylor BRADFORD

Catherine COOKSON

Maisie MOSCO

Belva PLAIN

Danielle STEEL

Helen VAN SLYKE

Marilyn FRENCH
General

Lisa ALTHER

Margaret DRABBLE

Alison LURIE

Ann OAKLEY

Edna O'BRIEN

Marge PIERCY

Judith ROSSNER

Anne TYLER

Brian FREEMANTLE
Adventure

Ted ALLBEURY

Jon CLEARY

Len DEIGHTON

Ian FLEMING

Frederick FORSYTH

John GARDNER

Philip FRIEDMAN
Crime

William J. COUGHLIN

John GRISHAM

Steve MARTINI

Scott TUROW

Rosemary FRIEDMAN
General

Rachel BILLINGTON

Elizabeth Jane HOWARD

Gillian TINDALL

Janet NEEL

Ruth RENDELL

Annette ROOME

Scott TUROW

Sara WOODS

Alexander FULLERTON
Adventure

Desmond BAGLEY

Brian CALLISON

Jon CLEARY

Bernard CORNWELL

John HARRIS

Max HENNESSY

Hammond INNES

Alistair MACLEAN

Dudley POPE

Douglas SCOTT

Elizabeth GAGE
The 'Smart Set'

Sally BEAUMAN

Sandra BROWN

Julie BURCHILL

Jackie COLLINS

Joan COLLINS

Jilly COOPER

Judith GOULD

Molly PARKIN

Harold ROBBINS

June Flaum SINGER

Frances FYFIELD
Crime

Linda BARNES

James M. CAIN

Sarah CAUDWELL

Patricia D. CORNWELL

Elizabeth GEORGE

Frances HEGARTY

P.D. JAMES

Steve MARTINI

Neil GAIMAN
Fantasy

Clive BARKER

Jamie DELANO

Dave GIBBONS

Frank MILLER

Alan MOORE

John WAGNER

Patrick GALE
General

Michael CARSON

Alan HOLLINGHURST

Paul MICOU

Stephen GALLAGHER
Supernatural

James HERBERT

Peter JAMES

Stephen KING

Dean R. KOONTZ

Mark MORRIS

Paul GALLICO
General

H.E. BATES

Monica DICKENS

Winston GRAHAM

Graham GREENE

Nevil SHUTE

Janice GALLOWAY
General

Sally EMERSON

Doris LESSING

John GALSWORTHY
General

Phyllis BENTLEY

F. Scott FITZGERALD

Winston GRAHAM

D.H. LAWRENCE

J.B. PRIESTLEY

Jane GARDAM
General

Hilary BAILEY

Susan HILL

Ursula HOLDEN

Jennifer JOHNSTON

Jane ROGERS

Muriel SPARK

William TREVOR

Mary WESLEY

Erle Stanley GARDNER
Crime

John Dickson CARR

Raymond CHANDLER

Ed McBAIN

Dell SHANNON

Rex STOUT

John GARDNER
Adventure

Eric AMBLER
Jeffrey ARCHER
Desmond BAGLEY
Leslie CHARTERIS
Len DEIGHTON
Ian FLEMING
Brian FREEMANTLE
Adam HALL
Palma HARCOURT
Jack HIGGINS
Hammond INNES
John LE CARRÉ
Gavin LYALL
Julian RATHBONE
John TRENHAILE

Jonathan GASH
Crime

Robert BARNARD
Simon BRETT
W.J. BURLEY
Colin DEXTER
Tim HEALD
Peter LOVESEY
James MELVILLE
Magdalen NABB
Iain PEARS
Neville STEED
David WILLIAMS

Catherine GASKIN
Historical

Teresa CRANE
Margaret ERSKINE
Judith GLOVER
Winston GRAHAM
Jane Aiken HODGE
Victoria HOLT
Susan HOWATCH
Claire LORRIMER
Pamela OLDFIELD
Diane PEARSON
Mary STEWART
E.V. THOMPSON

David GATES
General

John UPDIKE

Catherine GAVIN
Historical

Evelyn ANTHONY
Catherine COOKSON
Daphne DU MAURIER
Winston GRAHAM
Pamela HILL
Olivia MANNING
Philippa WIAT
Sarah WOODHOUSE

Michael GELLER
Crime

Dick FRANCIS

John FRANCOME

David A. GEMMELL
Fantasy

Ray BRADBURY

Marion Zimmer BRADLEY

Stephen KING

Mary GENTLE
Science Fiction

Ursula LE GUIN

Christopher PRIEST

Catherine GEORGE
Romance

Charlotte LAMB

Carole MORTIMER

Jessica STEELE

Elizabeth GEORGE
Crime

Agatha CHRISTIE

Amanda CROSS

Colin DEXTER

Antonia FRASER

Frances FYFIELD

Martha GRIMES

John HARVEY

P.D. JAMES

Ngaio MARSH

Sara PARETSKY

Ruth RENDELL

Patricia WENTWORTH

Margaret YORKE

Valerie GEORGESON
Historical

Philippa CARR

Christine Marion FRASER

Iris GOWER

Pamela OLDFIELD

Dave GIBBONS
Fantasy

Clive BARKER

Jamie DELANO

Neil GAIMAN

Stephen KING

Frank MILLER

Alan MOORE

William GIBSON
Science Fiction

David BRIN

John BRUNNER

William GIBSON (cont.)

Pat CADIGAN

Philip K. DICK

Bruce STERLING

Celia FREMLIN

Patricia HIGHSMITH

Charles GIDLEY
Family Stories

Malcolm MACDONALD

Caroline STICKLAND

Vivian STUART

Michael GILBERT
Crime

John Dickson CARR

Agatha CHRISTIE

Tim HEALD

John SHERWOOD

Michael UNDERWOOD

Sara WOODS

Ellen GILCHRIST
General

Ellen DOUGLAS

William FAULKNER

B.M. GILL
Crime

W.J. BURLEY

Anthea COHEN

Judith GLOVER
Historical

Margaret ERSKINE

Catherine GASKIN

Anne MELVILLE

Rosamunde PILCHER

Judith SAXTON

Robert GODDARD
Adventure

Jeffrey ARCHER

Desmond BAGLEY

Dirk BOGARDE

John BUCHAN

Daphne DU MAURIER

Winston GRAHAM

Geoffrey HOUSEHOLD

Rumer GODDEN
General

R.F. DELDERFIELD

Monica DICKENS

Nadine GORDIMER

Ruth Prawer JHABVALA

Elizabeth JOLLEY

Olivia MANNING

John MASTERS

John MORTIMER

Maisie MOSCO

Diana STAINFORTH

Anne TYLER

Gail GODWIN
Family Stories

Belva PLAIN

Helen VAN SLYKE

William GOLDING
General

Anthony BURGESS

John FOWLES

Graham GREENE

Ernest HEMINGWAY

Thomas KENEALLY

Barry UNSWORTH

Patrick WHITE

Robert GOLDSBOROUGH
Crime

James Hadley CHASE

Rex STOUT

Suzanne GOODWIN
Family Stories

Virginia ANDREWS

Margaret GRAHAM

Nadine GORDIMER
General

Margaret ATWOOD

Lynne Reid BANKS

Nina BAWDEN

Andre BRINK

Brigid BROPHY

Joyce CARY

J.M. COETZEE

Buchi EMECHETA

Rumer GODDEN

Elspeth HUXLEY

Ruth Prawer JHABVALA

Doris LESSING

Toni MORRISON

Penelope MORTIMER

V.S. NAIPAUL

Ben OKRI

Joy PACKER

Alan PATON

Paul SCOTT

Patrick WHITE

Richard GORDON
Humour

H.E. BATES
E.F. BENSON
Colin DOUGLAS
Leslie THOMAS
P.G. WODEHOUSE

Elizabeth GOUDGE
General

Phyllis BENTLEY
Mazo DE LA ROCHE
Winston GRAHAM
Miss READ
Anya SETON
Elswyth THANE

Judith GOULD
The 'Smart Set'

Jackie COLLINS
Jilly COOPER
Elizabeth GAGE
Judith KRANTZ

Iris GOWER
Family Stories

Betty BURTON
Catherine COOKSON
Alexander CORDELL
Josephine COX
Margaret Thomson DAVIS
R.F. DELDERFIELD
Valerie GEORGESON
Brenda JAGGER
Marie JOSEPH
Sheelagh KELLY
Lena KENNEDY
Anne MELVILLE
Pamela OLDFIELD
Elvi RHODES
Janet TANNER
Grace THOMPSON

Sue GRAFTON
Crime

Linda BARNES
Liza CODY
Patricia D. CORNWELL
Amanda CROSS
Antonia FRASER
Ed McBAIN
Susan MOODY
Sara PARETSKY

Margaret GRAHAM
Family Stories

Catherine COOKSON
Suzanne GOODWIN
Diana STAINFORTH

Winston GRAHAM
General

R.F. DELDERFIELD

Daphne DU MAURIER

Robert GODDARD

Richard LLEWELLYN

Howard SPRING

Phyllis A. WHITNEY

Winston GRAHAM
Historical

Anita BURGH

Alexander CORDELL

Catherine GAVIN

Cynthia HARROD-EAGLES

Susan HOWATCH

Jessica STIRLING

E.V. THOMPSON

Ann GRANGER
Crime

Agatha CHRISTIE

Janet LAURENCE

C.F. ROE

Lesley GRANT-ADAMSON
Crime

Margery ALLINGHAM

Anthea COHEN

Antonia FRASER

P.D. JAMES

Sara PARETSKY

Ruth RENDELL

Günter GRASS
General

Isabel ALLENDE

David GROSSMAN

Herman HESSE

Gabriel Garcia MARQUEZ

Ben OKRI

Robert GRAVES
General

Gillian BRADSHAW

Colleen McCULLOUGH

Allan MASSIE

Mary RENAULT

Gore VIDAL

Alasdair GRAY
General

Anthony BURGESS

Salman RUSHDIE

Graham GREENE
General

Elizabeth BOWEN

William BOYD

Graham GREENE (cont.)

Joseph CONRAD
A.J. CRONIN
Lawrence DURRELL
F. Scott FITZGERALD
E.M. FORSTER
Paul GALLICO
William GOLDING
L.P. HARTLEY
Ernest HEMINGWAY
Aldous HUXLEY
Thomas KENEALLY
W. Somerset MAUGHAM
Stanley MIDDLETON
Brian MOORE
V.S. NAIPAUL
George ORWELL
Alan PATON
Anthony POWELL
Piers Paul READ
Irwin SHAW
C.P. SNOW
Paul THEROUX
William TREVOR
Evelyn WAUGH
Morris WEST
Angus WILSON

Colin GREENLAND
Fantasy

James P. BLAYCOCK
Robert HOLDSTOCK

D.M. GREENWOOD
Crime

P.C. DOHERTY
Ellis PETERS

Stephen GREGORY
General

John FOWLES
Barry UNSWORTH

Zane GREY
Western

Max BRAND
Al CODY
Wade HAMILTON
Louis L'AMOUR
Lauran PAINE

W.E.B. GRIFFIN
War

Peter ABRAHAMS
Larry FORRESTER
John HARRIS
Robert JACKSON

Derek ROBINSON

Terence STRONG

L.K. TRUSCOTT

Martha GRIMES
Crime

W.J. BURLEY

Agatha CHRISTIE

Elizabeth FERRARS

Antonia FRASER

Elizabeth GEORGE

P.D. JAMES

Gillian LINSCOTT

Patricia WENTWORTH

John GRISHAM
Crime

Patricia D. CORNWELL

William J. COUGHLIN

Michael CRICHTON

Philip FRIEDMAN

Steve MARTINI

Scott TUROW

David GROSSMAN
General

Günter GRASS

Primo LEVI

Chaim POTOK

Isaac Bashevis SINGER

George GROSSMITH
Humour

Jerome K. JEROME

Christopher MATTHEW

Nicholas GUILD
Adventure

J.K. MAYO

Elleston TREVOR

Rosa GUY
General

Marsha HUNT

Terry McMILLAN

Toni MORRISON

Alice WALKER

William HAGGARD
Adventure

Jeffrey ARCHER

John GARDNER

Geoffrey HOUSEHOLD

Arthur HAILEY
Adventure

Jeffrey ARCHER

Desmond BAGLEY

James CLAVELL

Richard CONDON

Richard COX

Henry DENKER

Ken FOLLETT

Frederick FORSYTH

Jack HIGGINS

Hammond INNES

Norman MAILER

Irwin SHAW

Sidney SHELDON

Frank G. SLAUGHTER

Wilbur SMITH

Leslie WALLER

Morris WEST

Joe HALDEMAN
Science Fiction

Poul ANDERSON

Isaac ASIMOV

Adam HALL
Adventure

Ted ALLBEURY

Eric AMBLER

David BRIERLEY

Len DEIGHTON

Ian FLEMING

John GARDNER

Derek LAMBERT

Robert LITTELL

Helen MACINNES

Owen SELA

Elleston TREVOR

James HALL
Crime

James Lee BURKE

Robert CRAIS

Carl HIAASEN

Elmore LEONARD

John D. MACDONALD

Rodney HALL
General

Peter CAREY

David MALOUF

Barbara HAMBLY
Fantasy

Andre NORTON

Robert B. PARKER

Ross THOMAS

Wade HAMILTON
Western

Max BRAND

Matt CHISHOLM

Zane GREY

Louis L'AMOUR

James HAMILTON-PATERSON
General

Ian COCHRANE

Ian McEWAN

Barbara HAMLYN
Historical

Gillian BRADSHAW

Elizabeth BYRD

Dashiell HAMMETT
Crime

William BAYER

Raymond CHANDLER

James Hadley CHASE

James ELLROY

Loren D. ESTLEMAN

Dan KAVANAGH

Elmore LEONARD

Ed McBAIN

Ross MACDONALD

Walter MOSLEY

Georgina HAMMICK
General

Nina BAWDEN

Isobel COLEGATE

Barbara COMYNS

Joanna TROLLOPE

Gerald HAMMOND
Crime

Celia FREMLIN

Michael UNDERWOOD

John WAINWRIGHT

Margaret YORKE

Rosemary HAMMOND
Romance

Lindsay ARMSTRONG

Penny JORDAN

Palma HARCOURT
Adventure

Ted ALLBEURY

Eric AMBLER

Evelyn ANTHONY

Tom CLANCY

Clive EGLETON

Palma HARCOURT (cont.)

Ken FOLLETT

Colin FORBES

John GARDNER

Robert LUDLUM

Helen MACINNES

Julian RATHBONE

Craig THOMAS

Raymond HARDIE
Sea

C.S. FORESTER

A.E. LANGSFORD

Patrick O'BRIAN

Clare HARKNESS
General

Joan AIKEN

Susan HILL

Elizabeth HARRIS
General

Joan AIKEN

Madeleine BRENT

John HARRIS
Adventure

Brian CALLISON

Tom CLANCY

James FOLLETT

Jack HIGGINS

Christopher HYDE

Duncan KYLE

A.E. LANGSFORD

Harry PATTERSON

Julian RATHBONE

John HARRIS
War

Alexander FULLERTON

Richard HOUGH

Robert JACKSON

Hans Helmut KIRST

Alistair MACLEAN

Nicholas MONSARRAT

Douglas REEMAN

Derek ROBINSON

Douglas SCOTT

Martyn HARRIS
General

Malcolm BRADBURY

Ben ELTON

Howard JACOBSON

Michael MALONE

Steve HARRIS
Supernatural

Ramsey CAMPBELL

Philip RICKMAN

Thomas HARRIS
Crime

John SANDFORD

Sidney SHELDON

David WILTSE

Harry HARRISON
Science Fiction

Douglas ADAMS

Brian W. ALDISS

Isaac ASIMOV

Ray BRADBURY

Larry NIVEN

Terry PRATCHETT

John WYNDHAM

M. John HARRISON
Fantasy

Robert BLOCH

Robert HOLDSTOCK

Ray HARRISON
Crime

Peter LOVESEY

Amy MYERS

Ellis PETERS

Julian SYMONS

M.J. TROW

Sarah HARRISON
Family Stories

Maeve BINCHY

R.F. DELDERFIELD

Susan HOWATCH

Maisie MOSCO

Wendy PERRIAM

Sarah HARRISON
The 'Smart Set'

Julie ELLIS

Elizabeth GAGE

Cynthia HARROD-EAGLES
Historical

Evelyn ANTHONY

Pamela BELLE

Philippa CARR

Emma DRUMMOND

Barbara ERSKINE

Cynthia HARROD-EAGLES (cont.)

Winston GRAHAM

Victoria HOLT

Rosalind LAKER

Anya SETON

Vivian STUART

E.V. THOMPSON

Patricia WENDORF

Stanley MIDDLETON

J.B. PRIESTLEY

C.P. SNOW

Howard SPRING

Roy HART
Crime

W.J. BURLEY

Douglas CLARK

Alan HUNTER

Michael HARTLAND
Adventure

Larry BOND

Robert CARTER

James CLAVELL

Eric VAN LUSTBADER

L.P. HARTLEY
General

H.E. BATES

John CHEEVER

F. Scott FITZGERALD

Graham GREENE

D.H. LAWRENCE

John HARVEY
Crime

Robert BARNARD

Colin DEXTER

Elizabeth GEORGE

Mark HEBDEN

Reginald HILL

Sheila RADLEY

Mike RIPLEY

R.D. WINGFIELD

Roy HATTERSLEY
General

John MORTIMER

A.N. WILSON

S.T. HAYMON
Crime

W.J. BURLEY

Janet NEEL

Ruth RENDELL

STAYNES & STOREY

Peter TURNBULL

Tim HEALD
Crime

Simon BRETT

Jonathan GASH

Michael GILBERT

Mark HEBDEN

Colin WATSON

Mark HEBDEN
Crime

Robert BARNARD

W.J. BURLEY

Nicolas FREELING

John HARVEY

Tim HEALD

Alan HUNTER

Roderic JEFFRIES

H.R.F. KEATING

Magdalen NABB

Georges SIMENON

John WAINWRIGHT

Frances HEGARTY
Crime

Mary Higgins CLARK

Frances FYFIELD

Jonathan KELLERMAN

Judith KELMAN

Barbara VINE

Robert A. HEINLEIN
Science Fiction

Brian W. ALDISS

Isaac ASIMOV

Ray BRADBURY

Arthur C. CLARKE

Philip K. DICK

John WYNDHAM

Joseph HELLER
General

Saul BELLOW

John IRVING

Ken KESEY

Philip ROTH

Leslie THOMAS

John UPDIKE

William WHARTON

Ernest HEMINGWAY
General

Erskine CALDWELL

Truman CAPOTE

Joseph CONRAD

William FAULKNER

William GOLDING

Graham GREENE

James JOYCE

Norman MAILER

John O'HARA

Ernest HEMINGWAY (cont.)

Ernest RAYMOND

Erich Maria REMARQUE

John STEINBECK

William STYRON

Paul THEROUX

Paul WATKINS

Max HENNESSY
War

Bernard CORNWELL

Alan EVANS

Larry FORRESTER

Alexander FULLERTON

John HARRIS

Christopher HYDE

Philip McCUTCHAN

Douglas REEMAN

Derek ROBINSON

Douglas SCOTT

John WINTON

Frank HERBERT
Science Fiction

Brian ALDISS

Isaac ASIMOV

Ray BRADBURY

Michael MOORCOCK

Jack VANCE

David WINGROVE

John WYNDHAM

James HERBERT
Supernatural

Jonathan AYCLIFFE

Ramsey CAMPBELL

Stephen GALLAGHER

Shaun HUTSON

Peter JAMES

Stephen KING

Dean R. KOONTZ

Stephen LAWS

Richard LAYMON

Graham MASTERTON

Philip RICKMAN

Guy N. SMITH

Herman HESSE
General

Saul BELLOW

Albert CAMUS

Günter GRASS

Jack KEROUAC

J.R.R. TOLKIEN

Georgette HEYER
Crime

Margery ALLINGHAM

Michael INNES

Ngaio MARSH

Gladys MITCHELL

Dorothy SAYERS

Dorothy SIMPSON

Georgette HEYER
Historical

Joan AIKEN

Elizabeth CHADWICK

Marion CHESNEY

Jane Aiken HODGE

Rosalind LAKER

Diana NORMAN

Carl HIAASEN
General

Ben ELTON

James HALL

John D. MACDONALD

Charles WILLEFORD

Jack HIGGINS
Adventure

Desmond BAGLEY

Larry BOND

John BUCHAN

Tom CLANCY

Nelson DE MILLE

Ken FOLLETT

Colin FORBES

Frederick FORSYTH

Clare FRANCIS

John GARDNER

Arthur HAILEY

John HARRIS

Hammond INNES

John LE CARRÉ

Alistair MACLEAN

Harry PATTERSON

Douglas SCOTT

Gerald SEYMOUR

Wilbur SMITH

Craig THOMAS

Elleston TREVOR

Patricia HIGHSMITH
Crime

Anthea COHEN

B.M. GILL

Ruth RENDELL

Simon SHAW

Julian SYMONS

Michael TOLKIN

Barbara VINE

Margaret YORKE

Pamela HILL
Historical

Catherine GAVIN

Jean PLAIDY

Philippa WIAT

Porter HILL
Sea

Ronald BASSETT

Alexander KENT

Richard WOODMAN

Reginald HILL
Crime

Campbell ARMSTRONG

W.J. BURLEY

Colin DEXTER

John HARVEY

Bill JAMES

Philip KERR

Bill KNOX

James McCLURE

Jonathan ROSS

John WAINWRIGHT

R.D. WINGFIELD

Susan HILL
General

Joan AIKEN

Beryl BAINBRIDGE

Margaret DRABBLE

Daphne DU MAURIER

Margaret FORSTER

Jane GARDAM

Clare HARKNESS

Jennifer JOHNSTON

Penelope LIVELY

Barbara PYM

Carol SHIELDS

Muriel SPARK

William TREVOR

Tony HILLERMAN
Crime

James Lee BURKE

Eugene IZZI

David L. LINDSEY

Ed McBAIN

Ellis PETERS

John Buxton HILTON
Crime

John CREASEY

Lindsey DAVIS

Peter LOVESEY

Chester B. HIMES
General

Tom KAKONIS

John Edgar WIDEMAN

Barry HINES
General

Truman CAPOTE

Carson McCULLERS

J.D. SALINGER

Burt HIRSCHFELD
The 'Smart Set'

Sally BEAUMAN

Harold ROBBINS

Jacqueline SUSANN

Mary HOCKING
General

Patricia ANGADI

Molly KEANE

Barbara PYM

Mary WESLEY

Jane Aiken HODGE
Historical

Daphne DU MAURIER

Catherine GASKIN

Winston GRAHAM

Georgette HEYER

Victoria HOLT

Claire LORRIMER

Jean PLAIDY

Anya SETON

Mary STEWART

Alice HOFFMAN
General

Lisa ALTHER

Jack KEROUAC

Alison LURIE

Carson McCULLERS

Anne TYLER

James P. HOGAN
Science Fiction

Greg BEAR

C.J. CHERRYH

Bob SHAW

Ursula HOLDEN
General

Jane GARDAM

Jennifer JOHNSTON

Robert HOLDSTOCK
Fantasy

James P. BLAYCOCK

August DERLETH

Robert BLOCH

Colin GREENLAND

M. John HARRISON

Keith ROBERTS

Gene WOLFE

Isabelle HOLLAND
Historical

Philippa CARR

Phyllis A. WHITNEY

Alan HOLLINGHURST
General

Michael CARSON

Patrick GALE

Adam MARS-JONES

Armistead MAUPIN

Edmund WHITE

Tom HOLT
Humour

H.E. BATES

Michael DOBBS

Garrison KEILLOR

P.G. WODEHOUSE

Tom HOLT
Science Fiction

Douglas ADAMS

Robert ADAMS

Terry PRATCHETT

Victoria HOLT
Historical

Madeleine BRENT

Philippa CARR

Emma DRUMMOND

Catherine GASKIN

Cynthia HARROD-EAGLES

Jane Aiken HODGE

Sara HYLTON

Rosalind LAKER

Claire LORRIMER

Carola SALISBURY

Anya SETON

Mary STEWART

Jessica STIRLING

Winifred HOLTBY
General

Phyllis BENTLEY

Lettice COOPER

Mazo DE LA ROCHE

Daphne DU MAURIER

Howard SPRING

Evelyn HOOD
Family Stories

Margaret Thomson DAVIS

Christine Marion FRASER

Nicola THORNE

Christopher HOPE
General

Andre BRINK

John FOWLES

Alan PATON

William HORWOOD
General

Richard ADAMS

Brian CARTER

Aeron CLEMENT

A.R. LLOYD

Brian PARVIN

Henry WILLIAMSON

Richard HOUGH
War

John HARRIS

Hans Helmut KIRST

Philip McCUTCHAN

Geoffrey HOUSEHOLD
Adventure

John BUCHAN

Robert GODDARD

David MASON

Audrey HOWARD
Family Stories

Tessa BARCLAY

Maeve BINCHY

Emma BLAIR

Catherine COOKSON

Frank DELANEY

Kate FLYNN

Helen FORRESTER

Marie JOSEPH

Lena KENNEDY

Beryl KINGSTON

Rosamunde PILCHER

Claire RAYNER

Jessica STIRLING

Elizabeth Jane HOWARD
General

Beryl BAINBRIDGE

Rachel BILLINGTON

Maeve BINCHY

A.S. BYATT

Kathleen CONLON

R.F. DELDERFIELD

Elizabeth Jane HOWARD (cont.)

Monica DICKENS

Margaret DRABBLE

Margaret FORSTER

Rosemary FRIEDMAN

Susan HOWATCH

Barbara PYM

Muriel SPARK

Elizabeth TAYLOR

Diane PEARSON

Jean STUBBS

Reay TANNAHILL

E.V. THOMPSON

Joanna TROLLOPE

Stephanie HOWARD
Romance

Penny JORDAN

Charlotte LAMB

Carole MORTIMER

Betty NEELS

Susan HOWATCH
Family Stories

Barbara Taylor BRADFORD

R.F. DELDERFIELD

Daphne DU MAURIER

Zoe FAIRBAIRNS

Christine Marion FRASER

Catherine GASKIN

Winston GRAHAM

Sarah HARRISON

Elizabeth Jane HOWARD

Christopher HUDSON
General

J.G. FARRELL

M.M. KAYE

W. Somerset MAUGHAM

Marsha HUNT
General

Rosa GUY

Terry McMILLAN

Timothy MO

Alice WALKER

Alan HUNTER
Crime

W.J. BURLEY

Roy HART

Mark HEBDEN

John WAINWRIGHT

David WILLIAMS

Shaun HUTSON
Supernatural

James HERBERT

Stephen KING

Richard LAYMON

Aldous HUXLEY
General

Graham GREENE

D.H. LAWRENCE

George ORWELL

Anthony POWELL

Evelyn WAUGH

Elspeth HUXLEY
General

Nadine GORDIMER

Doris LESSING

Christopher HYDE
Adventure

John HARRIS

Max HENNESSY

Geoffrey JENKINS

Sara HYLTON
Historical

Madeleine BRENT

Victoria HOLT

Marie JOSEPH

Margaret PEMBERTON

Carola SALISBURY

Hammond INNES
Adventure

Eric AMBLER

Desmond BAGLEY

John BUCHAN

Brian CALLISON

Victor CANNING

Jon CLEARY

Clive CUSSLER

Ken FOLLETT

C.S. FORESTER

Alexander FULLERTON

John GARDNER

Arthur HAILEY

Jack HIGGINS

Robert JACKSON

Geoffrey JENKINS

Duncan KYLE

Gavin LYALL

Helen MACINNES

Alistair MACLEAN

Nicholas MONSARRAT

Douglas REEMAN

Derek ROBINSON

Nevil SHUTE

Wilbur SMITH

Hammond INNES (cont.)

Elleston TREVOR

Antony TREW

Michael INNES
Crime

Margery ALLINGHAM

John Dickson CARR

Raymond CHANDLER

Edmund CRISPIN

Colin DEXTER

Dick FRANCIS

Georgette HEYER

Ngaio MARSH

Gladys MITCHELL

Dorothy L. SAYERS

Josephine TEY

John IRVING
General

Joseph HELLER

Ken KESEY

Larry McMURTRY

Irwin SHAW

John UPDIKE

Kazuo ISHIGURO
General

Russell BANKS

Julian BARNES

William BOYD

Shusako ENDO

Ronald FRAME

Thomas KENEALLY

Ian McEWAN

Yukio MISHIMA

Timothy MO

Haruki MURAKAMI

Vladimir NABOKOV

Eugene IZZI
Crime

Lesley EGAN

Tony HILLERMAN

Andrew VACHSS

Charles WILLEFORD

Robert JACKSON
War

W.E.B. GRIFFIN

John HARRIS

Hammond INNES

Howard JACOBSON
General

Malcolm BRADBURY

Martyn HARRIS

Malcolm MALONE

David NOBBS

Frederic RAPHAEL

Tom SHARPE

Rona JAFFE
General

Alison LURIE

Danielle STEEL

Brenda JAGGER
Family Stories

Tessa BARCLAY

Emma BLAIR

Barbara Taylor BRADFORD

Philippa CARR

Brenda CLARKE

Catherine COOKSON

Christine Marion FRASER

Iris GOWER

Winston GRAHAM

Sheelagh KELLY

Beryl KINGSTON

Pamela OLDFIELD

Kay STEPHENS

Jessica STIRLING

Bill JAMES
Crime

Reginald HILL

Dan KAVANAGH

James McCLURE

Henry JAMES
General

Joseph CONRAD

F. Scott FITZGERALD

E.M. FORSTER

D.H. LAWRENCE

Muriel SPARK

Edith WHARTON

P.D. JAMES
Crime

Margery ALLINGHAM

Colin DEXTER

Michael DIBDIN

Peter DICKINSON

Frances FYFIELD

Elizabeth GEORGE

Lesley GRANT-ADAMSON

Martha GRIMES

Jonathan KELLERMAN

Ruth RENDELL

Dorothy L. SAYERS

June THOMSON

Barbara VINE

Peter JAMES
Supernatural

Jonathan AYCLIFFE

Stephen GALLAGHER

James HERBERT

Stephen KING

Roderic JEFFRIES
Crime

Mark HEBDEN

Magdalen NABB

John WAINWRIGHT

Geoffrey JENKINS
Adventure

Desmond BAGLEY

Brian CALLISON

Jon CLEARY

Colin FORBES

Frederick FORSYTH

Clare FRANCIS

Christopher HYDE

Hammond INNES

Alexander KENT

Alistair MACLEAN

Douglas REEMAN

Nevil SHUTE

Wilbur SMITH

Robin JENKINS
General

George Mackay BROWN

Iain Crichton SMITH

Gary JENNINGS
Adventure

James CLAVELL

Nelson DE MILLE

Jerome K. JEROME
Humour

Augustus CARP

George GROSSMITH

A.G. MACDONELL

Christopher MATTHEW

Barry PAIN

P.G. WODEHOUSE

K.W. JETER
Science Fiction

Pat CADIGAN

Philip K. DICK

Rudy RUCKER

Ruth Prawer JHABVALA
General

Margaret ATWOOD

Anita DESAI

J.G. FARRELL

E.M. FORSTER

Rumer GODDEN

Nadine GORDIMER

John MASTERS

V.S. NAIPAUL

Paul SCOTT

Katherine JOHN
Crime

Jonathan KELLERMAN

Pamela Hansford JOHNSON
General

Olivia MANNING

Iris MURDOCH

C.P. SNOW

Muriel SPARK

Jennifer JOHNSTON
General

Beryl BAINBRIDGE

Alice Thomas ELLIS

Jane GARDAM

Susan HILL

Ursula HOLDEN

Molly KEANE

Penelope LIVELY

Brian MOORE

Iris MURDOCH

Edna O'BRIEN

Flann O'BRIEN

William TREVOR

Elizabeth JOLLEY
General

Angela CARTER

Rumer GODDEN

Hilary MANTEL

V.S. NAIPAUL

Gwyneth JONES
Science Fiction

Ursula LE GUIN

Grant NAYLOR

Mervyn JONES
General

Paul BAILEY

Stan BARSTOW

Lettice COOPER

David STOREY

Penny JORDAN
Romance

Lindsay ARMSTRONG

Barbara CARTLAND

Rosemary HAMMOND

Penny JORDAN (cont.)

Stephanie HOWARD

Charlotte LAMB

Anne MATHER

Carole MORTIMER

Annabel MURRAY

Betty NEELS

Lilian PEAKE

Jessica STEELE

Anne WEALE

Mary MINTON

Maisie MOSCO

Pamela OLDFIELD

Rosamunde PILCHER

Claire RAYNER

Miss READ

Elvi RHODES

Ann Victoria ROBERTS

Mary Jane STAPLES

Ted WILLIS

Robert JORDAN
Fantasy

David EDDINGS

Raymond E. FEIST

Marie JOSEPH
Family Stories

Tessa BARCLAY

Emma BLAIR

Catherine COOKSON

Josephine COX

Margaret Thomson DAVIS

Helen FORRESTER

Sara FRASER

Iris GOWER

Audrey HOWARD

Sara HYLTON

Lena KENNEDY

Beryl KINGSTON

James JOYCE
General

Saul BELLOW

Ernest HEMINGWAY

D.H. LAWRENCE

Flann O'BRIEN

Frank O'CONNOR

Sean O'FAOLAIN

William TREVOR

Bob JUDD
Adventure

Douglas RUTHERFORD

Tom KAKONIS
Crime

James Lee BURKE

Chester B. HIMES

Joseph KOENIG

Michael PEARCE

Charles WILLEFORD

Stuart M. KAMINSKY
General

Andrew COBURN

James McCLURE

John KATZENBACH
Adventure

Clive EGLETON

Dan KAVANAGH
Crime

Dashiell HAMMETT

Reginald HILL

Guy Gavriel KAY
Fantasy

David EDDINGS

J.R.R. TOLKIEN

M.M. KAYE
General

Winston GRAHAM

Christopher HUDSON

Olivia MANNING

John MASTERS

Gita MEHTA

James A. MICHENER

Margaret MITCHELL

Diane PEARSON

Mary STEWART

Phyllis A. WHITNEY

Daphne WRIGHT

Molly KEANE
General

Maeve BINCHY

Elizabeth BOWEN

Kathleen CONLON

Alice Thomas ELLIS

Mary HOCKING

Jennifer JOHNSTON

Edna O'BRIEN

Flann O'BRIEN

Barbara PYM

William TREVOR

Mary WESLEY

H.R.F. KEATING
Crime

Simon BRETT

W.J. BURLEY

John Dickson CARR

Raymond CHANDLER

Nicolas FREELING

H.R.F. KEATING (cont.)

Mark HEBDEN

James MELVILLE

Georges SIMENON

Michael UNDERWOOD

John WAINWRIGHT

Garrison KEILLOR
Humour

H.E. BATES

Ethan CANIN

Tom HOLT

William KENNEDY

Sinclair LEWIS

Gloria NAYLOR

Jonathan KELLERMAN
Crime

Mary Higgins CLARK

Patricia D. CORNWELL

Joy FIELDING

Frances HEGARTY

P.D. JAMES

Katherine JOHN

Judith KELMAN

Elmore LEONARD

Ed McBAIN

T. Jefferson PARKER

Ridley PEARSON

Lawrence SANDERS

Whitley STRIEBER

Sheelagh KELLY
Family Stories

Virginia ANDREWS

Maeve BINCHY

Emma BLAIR

Barbara Taylor BRADFORD

Iris GOWER

Brenda JAGGER

Adam KENNEDY

Susan KELLY
Crime

John SHERWOOD

James KELMAN
General

Roddy DOYLE

David STOREY

Judith KELMAN
Crime

Mary Higgins CLARK

Joy FIELDING

Frances HEGARTY

Jonathan KELLERMAN

Anita SHREVE

Thomas KENEALLY
General

William BOYD
Malcolm BRADBURY
Andre BRINK
Peter CAREY
E.L. DOCTOROW
William GOLDING
Graham GREENE
Kazuo ISHIGURO
David MALOUF
Brian MOORE
C.P. SNOW
Barry UNSWORTH

Adam KENNEDY
Family Stories

Barbara Taylor BRADFORD
Sheelagh KELLY

Lena KENNEDY
Family Stories

Emma BLAIR
Philip BOAST
Harry BOWLING
Catherine COOKSON
Josephine COX
Margaret Thomson DAVIS
Helen FORRESTER
Iris GOWER
Audrey HOWARD
Marie JOSEPH
Beryl KINGSTON
Connie MONK
Maisie MOSCO
Claire RAYNER
Susan SALLIS
Mary Jane STAPLES
Christine THOMAS
Ted WILLIS

William KENNEDY
General

John CHEEVER
E.L. DOCTOROW
Garrison KEILLOR

Alexander KENT
Sea

Ronald BASSETT
Brian CALLISON
Bernard CORNWELL
C.S. FORESTER
Porter HILL
Geoffrey JENKINS
A.E. LANGSFORD
Philip McCUTCHAN
Patrick O'BRIAN
Dudley POPE
Douglas REEMAN

Alexander KENT (cont.)

Victor SUTHREN

Peter TONKIN

Richard WOODMAN

Jack KEROUAC
General

Herman HESSE

Alice HOFFMAN

Jay McINERNEY

Larry McMURTRY

Katherine KERR
Fantasy

David EDDINGS

Anne McCAFFREY

Andre NORTON

Philip KERR
Adventure

Len DEIGHTON

Ian FLEMING

Nicolas FREELING

Reginald HILL

James McCLURE

Joe POYER

Georges SIMENON

Ken KESEY
General

Joseph HELLER

John IRVING

Paul SAYER

William KIENZLE
Crime

Michael CLYNES

Ellis PETERS

Garry D. KILWORTH
Fantasy

Robert ADAMS

Marion Zimmer BRADLEY

David EDDINGS

Tad WILLIAMS

Stephen KING
Fantasy

Clive BARKER

Orson Scott CARD

Stephen DONALDSON

Christopher FOWLER

David A. GEMMELL

Dave GIBBONS

Richard LAYMON

Anne McCAFFREY

Alan MOORE

Stephen KING
Supernatural

Jonathan AYCLIFF

Clive BARKER

Ramsey CAMPBELL

John FARRIS

Stephen GALLAGHER

James HERBERT

Shaun HUTSON

Peter JAMES

Dean R. KOONTZ

Robert McCAMMON

George R. MARTIN

Anne RICE

Dan SIMMONS

Peter STRAUB

Beryl KINGSTON
Family Stories

Maeve BINCHY

Emma BLAIR

Harry BOWLING

Brenda CLARKE

Josephine COX

Helen FORRESTER

Audrey HOWARD

Brenda JAGGER

Marie JOSEPH

Lena KENNEDY

Rosamunde PILCHER

Claire RAYNER

Elvi RHODES

Ann Victoria ROBERTS

Susan SALLIS

Judith SAXTON

Margaret SUNLEY

Reay TANNAHILL

E.V. THOMPSON

Nicola THORNE

Ted WILLIS

Hans Helmut KIRST
War

John HARRIS

Richard HOUGH

Bill KNOX
Crime

Reginald HILL

Peter TURNBULL

John WAINWRIGHT

Joseph KOENIG
Crime

James Lee BURKE

Tom KAKONIS

Andrew VACHSS

Arthur KOESTLER
General

George ORWELL

Dean R. KOONTZ
Supernatural

Jonathan AYCLIFFE
Ramsey CAMPBELL
John FARRIS
Stephen GALLAGHER
James HERBERT
Stephen KING
Richard LAYMON
Graham MASTERTON
Robert McCAMMON
Dan SIMMONS
Peter STRAUB
Whitley STRIEBER

Judith KRANTZ
The 'Smart Set'

Pat BOOTH
Jacqueline BRISKIN
Jackie COLLINS
Jilly COOPER
Julie ELLIS
Judith GOULD
Lynda LA PLANTE
Harold ROBBINS
Thomas TRYON

Milan KUNDERA
General

Isabel ALLENDE
William BOYD
Sebastian FAULKS
Ben OKRI

Hanif KUREISHI
General

Armistead MAUPIN
Timothy MO

Duncan KYLE
Adventure

Desmond BAGLEY
John BUCHAN
Brian CALLISON
Jon CLEARY
Frederick FORSYTH
Clare FRANCIS
John HARRIS
Hammond INNES
James LEASOR
Robert LUDLUM
Alistair MACLEAN
John MASTERS
Lawrence SANDERS

Rosalind LAKER
Historical

Pamela BELLE
Mazo DE LA ROCHE
Winston GRAHAM
Cynthia HARROD-EAGLES
Georgette HEYER
Victoria HOLT
Norah LOFTS
Jean PLAIDY
E.V. THOMPSON

Charlotte LAMB
Romance

Iris BROMIGE
Janet DAILEY
Joyce DINGWELL
Jane DONNELLY
Catherine GEORGE
Stephanie HOWARD
Penny JORDAN
Audrie MANLEY-TUCKER
Anne MATHER
Carole MORTIMER
Betty NEELS
Jessica STEELE
Kay THORPE

Derek LAMBERT
Adventure

Jon CLEARY
Len DEIGHTON
Frederick FORSYTH
Adam HALL
John LE CARRÉ
Robert LUDLUM

Louis L'AMOUR
Western

Max BRAND
Matt CHISHOLM
Al CODY
Jess CODY
J.T. EDSON
Zane GREY
Wade HAMILTON
John JAKES
Chuck MARTIN
Nelson NYE
Clint OGDEN
T.C. OLSEN
Lauran PAINE
Gary PAULSEN
Jack SCHAEFER
Bill WADE

Dinah LAMPITT
Historical

Philippa CARR

Diana NORMAN

A.E. LANGSFORD
Sea

C.S. FORESTER

Raymond HARDIE

John HARRIS

Alexander KENT

Philip McCUTCHAN

Alistair MACLEAN

Nicholas MONSARRAT

Douglas SCOTT

Lynda LA PLANTE
The 'Smart Set'

Pat BOOTH

Celia BRAYFIELD

Jackie COLLINS

Julie ELLIS

Judith KRANTZ

Molly PARKIN

Penny VINCENZI

Emma LATHEN
Crime

Margery ALLINGHAM

Agatha CHRISTIE

Amanda CROSS

Elizabeth FERRARS

Anne MORICE

Emma PAGE

Patricia WENTWORTH

Janet LAURENCE
Crime

Ann GRANGER

C.F. ROE

Annette ROOME

John SHERWOOD

David WILLIAMS

D.H. LAWRENCE
General

Stan BARSTOW

Melvyn BRAGG

E.M. FORSTER

John FOWLES

John GALSWORTHY

L.P. HARTLEY

Aldous HUXLEY

Henry JAMES

James JOYCE
Richard LLEWELLYN
Alan SILLITOE
David STOREY

Stephen LAWS
Fantasy

Robert ADAMS
James HERBERT
Mary STANTON

Richard LAYMON
Supernatural

James HERBERT
Shaun HUTSON
Stephen KING
Dean R. KOONTZ
Graham MASTERTON
Guy N. SMITH

James LEASOR
Adventure

Desmond BAGLEY
Francis CLIFFORD
Duncan KYLE
Nevil SHUTE

John LE CARRÉ
Adventure

Francis CLIFFORD
Richard CONDON
Len DEIGHTON
Clive EGLETON
Ken FOLLETT
Colin FORBES
Frederick FORSYTH
Brian FREEMANTLE
John GARDNER
Jack HIGGINS
Derek LAMBERT
Robert LITTELL
Anthony PRICE
Julian Jay SAVARIN
Tim SEBASTIAN
Gerald SEYMOUR
John TRENHAILE

Harper LEE
General

Carson McCULLERS
Bobbie Ann MASON
Joyce Carol OATES
John STEINBECK

Ursula LE GUIN
Science Fiction

Ray BRADBURY
Arthur C. CLARKE
Mary GENTLE
Gwyneth JONES
Doris LESSING
Vonda N. MACINTYRE
Andre NORTON
Marge PIERCY
Joanna RUSS
Robert SILVERBERG
Sheri S. TEPPER
Gene WOLFE

Rosamond LEHMANN
General

Elizabeth BOWEN
Olivia MANNING
Iris MURDOCH
Elizabeth TAYLOR
Rebecca WEST

Fritz LEIBER
Fantasy

Michael MOORCOCK
C.L. MOORE
Gene WOLFE

Stanislaw LEM
Science Fiction

Orson Scott CARD
Arthur C. CLARKE
Larry NIVEN
Eric Frank RUSSELL
Bob SHAW

Elizabeth LEMARCHAND
Crime

Marian BABSON
Pat BURDEN
Agatha CHRISTIE
Ngaio MARSH
Anne MORICE
Patricia MOYES
Emma PAGE
Patricia WENTWORTH

Elmore LEONARD
Crime

William BAYER
James Lee BURKE
Robert CAMPBELL
Robert CRAIS
Michael DIBDIN
James ELLROY
Loren D. ESTLEMAN

James HALL

Dashiell HAMMETT

Jonathan KELLERMAN

Ed McBAIN

Ross MACDONALD

Robert PARKER

Charles WILLEFORD

Doris LESSING
General

Beryl BAINBRIDGE

Joyce CARY

Janice GALLOWAY

Nadine GORDIMER

Elspeth HUXLEY

Ursula LE GUIN

Olivia MANNING

Candia McWILLIAM

Penelope MORTIMER

Iris MURDOCH

Joyce Carol OATES

Joy PACKER

Alan PATON

Christopher PRIEST

Paul SCOTT

Muriel SPARK

Primo LEVI
General

Saul BELLOW

David GROSSMAN

Amos OZ

Isaac Bashevis SINGER

C.S. LEWIS
Fantasy

H.P. LOVECRAFT

Mervyn PEAKE

J.R.R. TOLKIEN

Sinclair LEWIS
General

F. Scott FITZGERALD

Ford Maddox FORD

Garrison KEILLOR

David L. LINDSEY
Crime

William BAYER

James Lee BURKE

Tony HILLERMAN

John SANDFORD

Gillian LINSCOTT
Crime

Martha GRIMES

Gwen MOFFAT

Patricia WENTWORTH

Robert LITTELL
Adventure

Eric AMBLER

Adam HALL

John LE CARRÉ

Owen SELA

Christopher SHERLOCK

Penelope LIVELY
General

Nina BAWDEN

Rachel BILLINGTON

Anita BROOKNER

A.S. BYATT

Monica DICKENS

Margaret DRABBLE

Alice Thomas ELLIS

Penelope FITZGERALD

Margaret FORSTER

Susan HILL

Jennifer JOHNSTON

Stanley MIDDLETON

Deborah MOGGACH

Barbara PYM

Muriel SPARK

Gillian TINDALL

Fay WELDON

Caroline LLEWELLYN
General

Barbara MICHAELS

Mary STEWART

Phyllis A. WHITNEY

Richard LLEWELLYN
General

Phyllis BENTLEY

George Mackay BROWN

Alexander CORDELL

A.J. CRONIN

Winston GRAHAM

D.H. LAWRENCE

Howard SPRING

Sam LLEWELLYN
Sea

Bernard CORNWELL

Philip McCUTCHAN

Anthony TREW

John WINGATE

A.R. LLOYD
General

Robert ADAMS

Brian CARTER

William HORWOOD

Henry WILLIAMSON

Morgan LLYWELYN
Historical

Valerie ANAND

Diana NORMAN

Edith PARGETER

Sharon PENMAN

Rosemary SUTCLIFF

David LODGE
General

Kingsley AMIS

Martin AMIS

William BOYD

Malcolm BRADBURY

Michael DOBBS

Alison LURIE

Stanley MIDDLETON

John MORTIMER

David NOBBS

Tom SHARPE

Alan SILLITOE

Leslie THOMAS

Keith WATERHOUSE

Norah LOFTS
General

Elizabeth CHADWICK

Monica DICKENS

Daphne DU MAURIER

Georgette HEYER

Rosalind LAKER

Diana NORMAN

Jean PLAIDY

Anya SETON

Marguerite STEEN

Claire LORRIMER
Family Stories

Charlotte Vale ALLEN

Tessa BARCLAY

Emma BLAIR

Philippa CARR

Catherine COOKSON

Catherine GASKIN

Jane Aiken HODGE

Victoria HOLT

Danielle STEEL

H.P. LOVECRAFT
Fantasy

James P. BLAYCOCK

Robert BLOCH

Ray BRADBURY

Ramsey CAMPBELL

H.P. LOVECRAFT (cont.)

August DERLETH

C.S. LEWIS

Brian LUMLEY

Richard MATHESON

Mervyn PEAKE

Clark Ashton SMITH

Peter LOVESEY
Crime

Colin DEXTER

Jonathan GASH

Ray HARRISON

John Buxton HILTON

Ellis PETERS

Julian SYMONS

Michael UNDERWOOD

Nicholas LUARD
Fantasy

Jean M. AUEL

Elizabeth M. THOMAS

Russell LUCAS
General

Anita DESAI

Gita MEHTA

R.K. NARAYAN

Robert LUDLUM
Adventure

Ted ALLBEURY

Victor CANNING

Tom CLANCY

Francis CLIFFORD

Clive EGLETON

Ian FLEMING

James FOLLETT

Ken FOLLETT

Palma HARCOURT

Duncan KYLE

Derek LAMBERT

Harry PATTERSON

Julian RATHBONE

Lawrence SANDERS

Gerald SEYMOUR

Sidney SHELDON

Eric VAN LUSTBADER

Brian LUMLEY
Fantasy

James P. BLAYCOCK

H.P. LOVECRAFT

Richard MATHESON

Alison LURIE
General

Nina BAWDEN

Rachel BILLINGTON

Anita BROOKNER
Margaret DRABBLE
Louise ERDRICH
Margaret FORSTER
Marilyn FRENCH
Alice HOFFMAN
Rona JAFFE
David LODGE
Mary McCARTHY
Carson McCULLERS
John O'HARA
Jane ROGERS
Carol SHIELDS
Anne TYLER
Fay WELDON

Gavin LYALL
Adventure

Jon CLEARY
Len DEIGHTON
Ian FLEMING
Frederick FORSYTH
Brian FREEMANTLE
John GARDNER
Hammond INNES
Helen MACINNES
Alistair MACLEAN
Gerald SEYMOUR
Wilbur SMITH
Terence STRONG
Craig THOMAS

Genevieve LYONS
Historical

Evelyn ANTHONY
Teresa CRANE
Mary MINTON

Ed McBAIN
Crime

John Newton CHANCE
James Hadley CHASE
K.C. CONSTANTINE
John CREASEY
Lesley EGAN
Nicolas FREELING
Erle Stanley GARDNER
Sue GRAFTON
Dashiell HAMMETT
Tony HILLERMAN
Jonathan KELLERMAN
Elmore LEONARD
John D. MACDONALD
Sara PARETSKY
Robert B. PARKER
Dell SHANNON
Peter TURNBULL
Joseph WAMBAUGH

Patrick McCABE
General

Julian BARNES

Bruce CHATWIN

Paul MICOU

Anne McCAFFREY
Fantasy

Marion Zimmer BRADLEY

C.J. CHERRYH

David EDDINGS

Raymond E. FEIST

Katherine KERR

Stephen KING

Andre NORTON

Melanie RAWN

Christopher STASHEFF

Sheri S. TEPPER

Tad WILLIAMS

Janny WURTS

Robert McCAMMON
Supernatural

Jonathan AYCLIFFE

Clive BARKER

John FARRIS

Stephen KING

Dean R. KOONTZ

Graham MASTERTON

Mary McCARTHY
General

Alison LURIE

Edna O'BRIEN

Flannery O'CONNOR

William WHARTON

James McCLURE
Crime

Michael DIBDIN

Reginald HILL

Bill JAMES

Stuart M. KAMINSKY

Philip KERR

James MELVILLE

Magdalen NABB

Michael PEARCE

Carson McCULLERS
General

Erskine CALDWELL

Truman CAPOTE

F. Scott FITZGERALD

Barry HINES

Alice HOFFMAN

Harper LEE

Alison LURIE

Flannery O'CONNOR

J.D. SALINGER

Colleen McCULLOUGH
General

John Gordon DAVIS

Robert GRAVES

Malcolm MACDONALD

Margaret MITCHELL

Danielle STEEL

Marguerite STEEN

Vivian STUART

Eileen TOWNSEND

Philip McCUTCHAN
Sea

Ronald BASSETT

Brian CALLISON

John HARRIS

Max HENNESSY

Richard HOUGH

Alexander KENT

A.E. LANGSFORD

Sam LLEWELLYN

Alistair MACLEAN

Dudley POPE

Douglas REEMAN

Peter TONKIN

Antony TREW

John WINGATE

John WINTON

Richard WOODMAN

John D. MACDONALD
Crime

James M. CAIN

Raymond CHANDLER

James Hadley CHASE

James HALL

Carl HIAASEN

Ed McBAIN

Charles WILLEFORD

Malcolm MACDONALD
Family Stories

Noel BARBER

Alexander CORDELL

Charles GIDLEY

Winston GRAHAM

Colleen McCULLOUGH

Pamela OLDFIELD

Caroline STICKLAND

Vivian STUART

E.V. THOMPSON

Patricia WENDORF

Ross MACDONALD
Crime

Dashiell HAMMETT

Elmore LEONARD

Ross THOMAS

A.G. MACDONELL
Humour

E.F. BENSON

Augustus CARP

Henry CECIL

Jerome K. JEROME

P.G. WODEHOUSE

Ian McEWAN
General

Martin AMIS

Paul BAILEY

Beryl BAINBRIDGE

Julian BARNES

Ian COCHRANE

David COOK

James HAMILTON-PATERSON

Kazuo ISHIGURO

Brian MOORE

Iris MURDOCH

Piers Paul READ

Graham SWIFT

Colin THUBRON

John McGAHERN
General

John BANVILLE

Bernard MACLAVERTY

Brian MOORE

V.S. PRITCHETT

William TREVOR

Dan McGIRT
Fantasy

Robert ASPRIN

Terry PRATCHETT

Christopher STASHEFF

Jay McINERNEY
General

Jack KEROUAC

Philip ROTH

Tom WOLFE

Helen MACINNES
Adventure

Ted ALLBEURY

Evelyn ANTHONY

Desmond BAGLEY

David BRIERLEY

John BUCHAN

Colin FORBES

Clare FRANCIS

Brian FREEMANTLE

Adam HALL

Palma HARCOURT

Hammond INNES

Gavin LYALL

Anthony PRICE

Gerald SEYMOUR

Mary STEWART

Vonda N. MACINTYRE
Science Fiction

Arthur C. CLARKE

Richard COWPER

Ursula LE GUIN

Larry NIVEN

Shena MACKAY
General

Beryl BAINBRIDGE

Elizabeth PALMER

Barbara PYM

Hilda McKENZIE
Family Stories

Harry BOWLING

Mary MINTON

Janet TANNER

Rosie THOMAS

Bernard MACLAVERTY
General

John BANVILLE

John McGAHERN

Alistair MACLEAN
Adventure

Desmond BAGLEY

Victor CANNING

Jon CLEARY

Clive CUSSLER

Clive EGLETON

James FOLLETT

Ken FOLLETT

Alexander FULLERTON

John HARRIS

Jack HIGGINS

Hammond INNES

Geoffrey JENKINS

Duncan KYLE

A.E. LANGSFORD

Gavin LYALL

Philip McCUTCHAN

Nicholas MONSARRAT

Harry PATTERSON

Wilbur SMITH

Terry McMILLAN
General

Rosa GUY

Marsha HUNT

Toni MORRISON

Alice WALKER

Mary McMULLEN
Crime

Jessica MANN

Martin RUSSELL

Margaret YORKE

Larry McMURTRY
General

John IRVING

Jack KEROUAC

Marge PIERCY

John UPDIKE

Judith McNAUGHT
Romance

Anne MATHER

Betty NEELS

Kay THORPE

Elisabeth McNEILL
Family Stories

Emma BLAIR

Elvi RHODES

Sarah SHEARS

Candia McWILLIAM
General

A.S. BYATT

Sally EMERSON

Doris LESSING

Jane ROGERS

Marina WARNER

Norman MAILER
General

Saul BELLOW

Arthur HAILEY

Ernest HEMINGWAY

John STEINBECK

William STYRON

John UPDIKE

Tom WOLFE

Bernard MALAMUD
General

Philip ROTH

Isaac Bashevis SINGER

Michael MALONE
General

Ben ELTON

Martyn HARRIS

Howard JACOBSON

David MALOUF
General

Peter CAREY

Rodney HALL

Thomas KENEALLY

Morris WEST

Audrie MANLEY-TUCKER
Romance

Charlotte LAMB

Carole MORTIMER

Jessica STEELE

Jessica MANN
Crime

Mary McMULLEN

Paul MYERS

Margaret YORKE

Olivia MANNING
General

Lynne Reid BANKS

Rachel BILLINGTON

Elizabeth BOWEN

Margaret DRABBLE

Lawrence DURRELL

Margaret FORSTER

Catherine GAVIN

Rumer GODDEN

Pamela Hansford JOHNSON

M.M. KAYE

Rosamond LEHMANN

Doris LESSING

Penelope MORTIMER

Paul SCOTT

Elizabeth TAYLOR

Rebecca WEST

Hilary MANTEL
General

Hilary BAILEY

Elizabeth JOLLEY

Deborah MOGGACH

Mary WESLEY

Catherine MARCHANT
Family Stories

Harry BOWLING

Catherine COOKSON

Josephine COX

Gabriel Garcia MARQUEZ
General

Anthony BURGESS

Günter GRASS

Salman RUSHDIE

Adam MARS-JONES
General

Michael CARSON

Alan HOLLINGHURST

Ngaio MARSH
Crime

Margery ALLINGHAM

Josephine BELL

John Dickson CARR

Agatha CHRISTIE

Edmund CRISPIN

Elizabeth FERRARS

Elizabeth GEORGE

Georgette HEYER

Michael INNES

Elizabeth LEMARCHAND

Gladys MITCHELL

Patricia MOYES

Dorothy L. SAYERS

Dorothy SIMPSON

June THOMSON

Patricia WENTWORTH

Chuck MARTIN
Western

Jess CODY

Louis L'AMOUR

George R. MARTIN
Supernatural

Nancy COLLINS

Stephen KING

Graham MASTERTON

Anne RICE

Steve MARTINI
Crime

Philip FRIEDMAN

Frances FYFIELD

John GRISHAM

Scott TUROW

Bobbie Ann MASON
General

William FAULKNER

Harper LEE

Anne TYLER

David MASON
Adventure

Frederick FORSYTH

Geoffrey HOUSEHOLD

Allan MASSIE
General

Robert GRAVES

Frederic RAPHAEL

Piers Paul READ

Mary RENAULT

Rosemary SUTCLIFF

Gore VIDAL

John MASTERS
General

Victor CANNING

Amit CHAUDHURI

James CLAVELL

Jon CLEARY

J.G. FARRELL

E.M. FORSTER

Rumer GODDEN

Ruth Prawer JHABVALA

M.M. KAYE

Duncan KYLE

James A. MICHENER

V.S. NAIPAUL

R.K. NARAYAN

Paul SCOTT

Nevil SHUTE

Elleston TREVOR

Morris WEST

Graham MASTERTON
Supernatural

Ramsey CAMPBELL

Christopher FOWLER

James HERBERT

Dean KOONTZ

Richard LAYMON

Robert McCAMMON

George R. MARTIN

Mark MORRIS

Kim NEWMAN

John SAUL

Dennis WHEATLEY

Anne MATHER
Romance

Lucilla ANDREWS

Janet DAILEY

Joyce DINGWELL

Jane DONNELLY

Penny JORDAN

Charlotte LAMB

Judith McNAUGHT

Carole MORTIMER

Betty NEELS

Elizabeth SEIFERT

Jessica STEELE

Kay THORPE

Richard MATHESON
Fantasy

Ray BRADBURY

H.P. LOVECRAFT

Brian LUMLEY

Tom REAMY

Christopher MATTHEW
Humour

George GROSSMITH

Jerome K. JEROME

Keith WATERHOUSE

W. Somerset MAUGHAM
General

Joseph CONRAD

Graham GREENE

Christopher HUDSON

Howard SPRING

Morris WEST

Armistead MAUPIN
General

Truman CAPOTE

Alan HOLLINGHURST

Hanif KUREISHI

Julian MAY
Science Fiction

Michael MOORCOCK

Fred SABERHAGEN

Robert SILVERBERG

J.K. MAYO
Adventure

Peter DRISCOLL

Nicholas GUILD

Elleston TREVOR

Gita MEHTA
General

Amit CHAUDHURI

M.M. KAYE

Russell LUCAS

R.K. NARAYAN

Michael ONDAATJE

Salman RUSHDIE

Anne MELVILLE
Family Stories

Tessa BARCLAY

R.F. DELDERFIELD

Christine Marion FRASER

Judith GLOVER

Iris GOWER

Pamela OLDFIELD

Claire RAYNER

Sarah SHEARS

Jessica STIRLING

James MELVILLE
Crime

Jonathan GASH

H.R.F. KEATING

James McCLURE

Eric WRIGHT

Jennie MELVILLE
Crime

Gwendoline BUTLER

Antonia FRASER

Iain PEARS

Patricia WENTWORTH

Mary MELWOOD
Family Stories

Miss READ

D.E. STEVENSON

Essie SUMMERS

Angela THIRKELL

Barbara MICHAELS
General

Virginia ANDREWS

Mary Higgins CLARK

Virginia COFFMAN

Daphne DU MAURIER

Dorothy EDEN

Caroline LLEWELLYN

Elizabeth PETERS

Mary STEWART

Phyllis A. WHITNEY

Daoma WINSTON

James A. MICHENER
General

Noel BARBER

James CLAVELL

Nelson DE MILLE

Robert ELEGANT

M.M. KAYE

John MASTERS

Vikram SETH

Wilbur SMITH

Leon URIS

Gore VIDAL

Paul MICOU
General

Julian BARNES

William BOYD

Ronald FRAME

Patrick GALE

Patrick McCABE

Stanley MIDDLETON
General

Kingsley AMIS

Stan BARSTOW

Stanley MIDDLETON (cont.)

Melvyn BRAGG
David COOK
William COOPER
Graham GREENE
L.P. HARTLEY
Penelope LIVELY
David LODGE
Alan SILLITOE
David STOREY
William TREVOR

Frank MILLER
Fantasy

Jamie DELANO
Neil GAIMAN
Dave GIBBONS
Alan MOORE
John WAGNER

Sue MILLER
General

Ethan CANIN
Jon COHEN
Laurie COLWIN
Lorrie MOORE
Mary MORRIS
Anne TYLER

Mary MINTON
Family Stories

Marie JOSEPH
Genevieve LYONS
Hilda McKENZIE
Jessica STIRLING

Yukio MISHIMA
General

Russell BANKS
Shusako ENDO
Kazuo ISHIGURO

Gladys MITCHELL
Crime

Margery ALLINGHAM
John Dickson CARR
Agatha CHRISTIE
Edmund CRISPIN
Freeman Wills CROFTS
Georgette HEYER
Michael INNES
Ngaio MARSH
Gwen MOFFAT
John SHERWOOD
Patricia WENTWORTH

Margaret MITCHELL
Historical

M.M. KAYE

Colleen McCULLOUGH

Alexandra RIPLEY

Frank YERBY

Timothy MO
General

Julian BARNES

Marsha HUNT

Kazuo ISHIGURO

Hanif KUREISHI

Caryl PHILLIPS

Gwen MOFFAT
Crime

Margery ALLINGHAM

Gillian LINSCOTT

Gladys MITCHELL

John SHERWOOD

Patricia WENTWORTH

Deborah MOGGACH
General

Patricia ANGADI

A.S. BYATT

Anabel DONALD

Alice Thomas ELLIS

Anne FINE

Margaret FORSTER

Penelope LIVELY

Hilary MANTEL

Bel MOONEY

K.M. PEYTON

Gillian TINDALL

Fay WELDON

Connie MONK
Family Stories

Philip BOAST

Lena KENNEDY

Jessica STIRLING

Nicholas MONSARRAT
Sea

C.S. FORESTER

John HARRIS

Hammond INNES

A.E. LANGSFORD

Alistair MACLEAN

Douglas REEMAN

Nevil SHUTE

Susan MOODY
Crime

Linda BARNES

Simon BRETT

Susan MOODY (cont.)

Liza CODY
Sue GRAFTON
Sara PARETSKY
Mike RIPLEY

Bel MOONEY
General

Anabel DONALD
Anne FINE
Margaret FORSTER
Deborah MOGGACH
K.M. PEYTON

Michael MOORCOCK
Fantasy

Isaac ASIMOV
Hugh COOK
Samuel R. DELANY
Frank HERBERT
Fritz LEIBER
Julian MAY
C.L. MOORE
Christopher PRIEST
Bob SHAW
Robert SILVERBERG
Jack VANCE
Gene WOLFE

Alan MOORE
Fantasy

Clive BARKER
Jamie DELANO
Neil GAIMAN
Dave GIBBONS
Stephen KING
Frank MILLER
John WAGNER

Brian MOORE
General

Martin AMIS
Paul BAILEY
Julian BARNES
Saul BELLOW
William BOYD
David COOK
Graham GREENE
Jennifer JOHNSTON
Thomas KENEALLY
Ian McEWAN
John McGAHERN
Paul THEROUX
D.M. THOMAS
William TREVOR
Barry UNSWORTH

C.L. MOORE
Fantasy

Fritz LEIBER

Michael MOORCOCK

Lorrie MOORE
General

Louise ERDRICH

Sue MILLER

Anne TYLER

Catrin MORGAN
Family Stories

Philip BOAST

Jessica STIRLING

Anne MORICE
Crime

Pat BURDEN

Antonia FRASER

Emma LATHEN

Elizabeth LEMARCHAND

David WILLIAMS

Sara WOODS

Margaret YORKE

David MORRELL
Adventure

Alan SAVAGE

Don SILVERMAN

Richard STARK

Douglas TERMAN

Eric VAN LUSTBADER

Mark MORRIS
Supernatural

Stephen GALLAGHER

Graham MASTERTON

Mary MORRIS
General

Ethan CANIN

Jon COHEN

Sue MILLER

Toni MORRISON
General

Lisa ALTHER

James BALDWIN

E.L. DOCTOROW

Ralph ELLISON

Buchi EMECHETA

Nadine GORDIMER

Rosa GUY

Terry McMILLAN

Alice WALKER

Carole MORTIMER
Romance

Lindsay ARMSTRONG

Joyce DINGWELL

Jane DONNELLY

Catherine GEORGE

Stephanie HOWARD

Penny JORDAN

Charlotte LAMB

Audrie MANLEY-TUCKER

Anne MATHER

Betty NEELS

Jessica STEELE

Kay THORPE

John MORTIMER
Humour

Malcolm BRADBURY

Henry CECIL

Rumer GODDEN

Roy HATTERSLEY

David LODGE

Frederic RAPHAEL

Keith WATERHOUSE

Auberon WAUGH

Penelope MORTIMER
General

Beryl BAINBRIDGE

Margaret DRABBLE

Nadine GORDIMER

Doris LESSING

Olivia MANNING

Iris MURDOCH

Edna O'BRIEN

Muriel SPARK

Doris MORTMAN
Family Stories

Lewis ORDE

Margaret PEMBERTON

Belva PLAIN

Maisie MOSCO
Family Stories

Tessa BARCLAY

Harry BOWLING

Anita BURGH

Josephine COX

Rosemary ENRIGHT

Cynthia FREEMAN

Suzanne GOODWIN

Sarah HARRISON

Marie JOSEPH

Lena KENNEDY

Belva PLAIN

Claire RAYNER

Rosie THOMAS

Jan WEBSTER

Walter MOSLEY
Crime

James ELLROY

Dashiel HAMMETT

Charles WILLEFORD

Patricia MOYES
Crime

Margery ALLINGHAM

Elizabeth LEMARCHAND

Ngaio MARSH

Alice MUNRO
General

Edna O'BRIEN

Anne TYLER

Neil MUNRO
Historical

D.K. BROSTER

Elizabeth BYRD

Sharon PENMAN

Nigel TRANTER

Haruki MURAKAMI
General

Russell BANKS

Susako ENDO

Kazuo ISHIGURO

Yukio MISHIMA

Iris MURDOCH
General

Margaret ATWOOD

Elizabeth BOWEN

Brigid BROPHY

A.S. BYATT

Anita DESAI

Margaret DRABBLE

Janice ELLIOTT

Penelope FITZGERALD

Margaret FORSTER

John FOWLES

Pamela Hansford JOHNSON

Jennifer JOHNSTON

Rosamond LEHMANN

Doris LESSING

Ian McEWAN

Penelope MORTIMER

Joyce Carol OATES

Anthony POWELL

Bernice RUBENS

Emma TENNANT

Angus WILSON

Virginia WOOLF

Elizabeth MURPHY
Family Stories

Kate FLYNN

Helen FORRESTER

Nicola THORNE

Annabel MURRAY
Romance

Lindsay ARMSTRONG

Penny JORDAN

Lilian PEAKE

Anne WEALE

Amy MYERS
Crime

Ray HARRISON

Julian SYMONS

M.J. TROW

Paul MYERS
Crime

Dick FRANCIS

Jessica MANN

Richard RUSSELL

Magdalen NABB
Crime

Marian BABSON

Michael DIBDIN

Jonathan GASH

Mark HEBDEN

Roderic JEFFRIES

James McCLURE

Vladimir NABOKOV
General

Saul BELLOW

Kazuo ISHIGURO

John UPDIKE

V.S. NAIPAUL
General

Chinua ACHEBE

Saul BELLOW

Nadine GORDIMER

Graham GREENE

Ruth Prawer JHABVALA

Elizabeth JOLLEY

John MASTERS

Vikram SETH

Paul THEROUX

Patrick WHITE

R.K. NARAYAN
General

Amit CHAUDHURI

Anita DESAI

Russell LUCAS

John MASTERS

Gita MEHTA

Vikram SETH

Judith McNAUGHT

Anne MATHER

Carole MORTIMER

Jessica STEELE

Gloria NAYLOR
General

Ellen DOUGLAS

Garrison KEILLOR

Alice WALKER

Grant NAYLOR
Science Fiction

Douglas ADAMS

Gwyneth JONES

Terry PRATCHETT

Janet NEEL
Crime

Frances FYFIELD

S.T. HAYMON

Jonathan ROSS

Dorothy SIMPSON

Michael UNDERWOOD

Betty NEELS
Romance

Stephanie HOWARD

Penny JORDAN

Charlotte LAMB

Kim NEWMAN
Supernatural

Graham MASTERTON

Christopher NICOLE
Adventure

Martin BOOTH

James CLAVELL

Larry NIVEN
Science Fiction

Isaac ASIMOV

Arthur C. CLARKE

Harry HARRISON

Stanislaw LEM

Frederik POHL

David NOBBS
Humour

Kingsley AMIS

H.E. BATES

Guy BELLAMY

George Mackay BROWN

Roy CLARKE

David NOBBS (cont.)

Colin DOUGLAS
Roddy DOYLE
Michael FRAYN
Howard JACOBSON
David LODGE
Tom SHARPE
Alan SILLITOE
Leslie THOMAS
Peter TINNISWOOD
Keith WATERHOUSE
P.G. WODEHOUSE

Diana NORMAN
Historical

Evelyn ANTHONY
D.K. BROSTER
Philippa CARR
Dorothy DUNNETT
Georgette HEYER
Dinah LAMPITT
Morgan LLYWELYN
Norah LOFTS
Edith PARGETER
Jean PLAIDY
Judith M. RILEY
Rosemary SUTCLIFF

Andre NORTON
Fantasy

Raymond FEIST
Barbara HAMBLY
Katherine KERR
Ursula LE GUIN
Anne McCAFFREY
Sheri S. TEPPER
Janny WURTS

Nelson NYE
Western

Max BRAND
J.T. EDSON
Louis L'AMOUR

Robert NYE
General

Peter ACKROYD
John FOWLES
Barry UNSWORTH

Ann OAKLEY
General

Lisa ALTHER
Marilyn FRENCH
Judith ROSSNER

Joyce Carol OATES
General

Jenny DISKI
Harper LEE
Doris LESSING
Iris MURDOCH
Edna O'BRIEN

Patrick O'BRIAN
Sea

Ronald BASSETT
Gillian BRADSHAW
Joseph CONRAD
Bernard CORNWELL
C.S. FORESTER
Raymond HARDIE
Alexander KENT
Dudley POPE
Douglas REEMAN
Showell STYLES
Victor SUTHREN

Edna O'BRIEN
General

Lynne Reid BANKS
Maeve BINCHY
Clare BOYLAN
Brigid BROPHY
Margaret DRABBLE
Alice Thomas ELLIS
Marilyn FRENCH
Jennifer JOHNSTON
Molly KEANE
Mary McCARTHY
Penelope MORTIMER
Alice MUNRO
Joyce Carol OATES
Wendy PERRIAM
William TREVOR
Fay WELDON
Antonia WHITE

Flann O'BRIEN
General

J.P. DONLEAVY
J.G. FARRELL
Jennifer JOHNSTON
James JOYCE
Mollie KEANE

Flannery O'CONNOR
General

Mary McCARTHY
Carson McCULLERS
J.D. SALINGER

Frank O'CONNOR
General

James JOYCE

Sean O'FAOLAIN

Sean O'FAOLAIN
General

James JOYCE

Frank O'CONNOR

John O'HARA
General

Saul BELLOW

John CHEEVER

F. Scott FITZGERALD

Ford Maddox FORD

Ernest HEMINGWAY

Alison LURIE

John UPDIKE

Clint OGDEN
Western

Louis L'AMOUR

T.C. OLSEN

Lauran PAINE

Ben OKRI
General

Chinua ACHEBE

Nadine GORDIMER

Günter GRASS

Milan KUNDERA

Caryl PHILLIPS

Marc OLDEN
Adventure

Martin BOOTH

Alan SAVAGE

Eric VAN LUSTBADER

Pamela OLDFIELD
Family Stories

Charlotte Vale ALLEN

Tessa BARCLAY

Emma BLAIR

Harry BOWLING

Janet DAILEY

Rosemary ENRIGHT

Helen FORRESTER

Catherine GASKIN

Valerie GEORGESON

Iris GOWER

Brenda JAGGER

Marie JOSEPH

Malcolm MACDONALD

Anne MELVILLE

Mary E. PEARCE

Susan SALLIS

Judith SAXTON

Janet TANNER

Nicola THORNE

Patricia WENDORF

Sarah WOODHOUSE

T.C. OLSEN
Western

Jess CODY

Louis L'AMOUR

Lauran PAINE

Gary PAULSEN

Michael ONDAATJE
General

Gita MEHTA

Salman RUSHDIE

Antony SHER

Lewis ORDE
Family Stories

Doris MORTMAN

Belva PLAIN

Anne Rivers SIDDONS

Rosie THOMAS

Judy TURNER

Roger ORMEROD
Crime

W.J. BURLEY

Colin DEXTER

Elizabeth FERRARS

Michael UNDERWOOD

George ORWELL
General

Anthony BURGESS

Graham GREENE

Aldous HUXLEY

Arthur KOESTLER

Amos OZ
General

Primo LEVI

Chaim POTOK

Isaac Bashevis SINGER

Joy PACKER
General

Monica DICKENS

Daphne DU MAURIER

Nadine GORDIMER

Doris LESSING

Marguerite STEEN

Mary STEWART

Emma PAGE
Crime

Pat BURDEN

Emma LATHEN

Elizabeth LEMARCHAND

Sara WOODS

Frances PAIGE
Family Stories

Lyn ANDREWS

Christine Marion FRASER

Sarah SHEARS

Jan WEBSTER

Dee WILLIAMS

Barry PAIN
Humour

Augustus CARP

Jerome K. JEROME

Lauran PAINE
Western

Zane GREY

Louis L'AMOUR

Clint OGDEN

T.C. OLSEN

Elizabeth PALMER
General

Shena MACKAY

Barbara PYM

Elizabeth TAYLOR

Sara PARETSKY
Crime

Linda BARNES

Raymond CHANDLER

Liza CODY

Antonia FRASER

Elizabeth GEORGE

Sue GRAFTON

Lesley GRANT-ADAMSON

Ed McBAIN

Susan MOODY

Joan SMITH

Edith PARGETER
Historical

Valerie ANAND

Dorothy DUNNETT

Morgan LLYWELYN

Diana NORMAN

Sharon PENMAN

Jean PLAIDY

Judith M. RILEY

Rosemary SUTCLIFF

Robert B. PARKER
Crime

Raymond CHANDLER

James Hadley CHASE

Andrew COBURN

Liza CODY

Dashiell HAMMETT

Elmore LEONARD

Ed McBAIN

T. Jefferson PARKER
Crime

Jonathan KELLERMAN

Dell SHANNON

Joseph WAMBAUGH

Una-Mary PARKER
Family Stories

John Gordon DAVIS

Danielle STEEL

Molly PARKIN
The 'Smart Set'

Sally BEAUMAN

Jackie COLLINS

Elizabeth GAGE

Lynda LA PLANTE

Brian PARVIN
General

Brian CARTER

Aeron CLEMENT

William HORWOOD

Henry WILLIAMSON

Alan PATON
General

James BALDWIN

Andre BRINK

Nadine GORDIMER

Graham GREENE

Christopher HOPE

Doris LESSING

Wilbur SMITH

John STEINBECK

Harry PATTERSON
Adventure

Jon CLEARY

Len DEIGHTON

Ian FLEMING

Frederick FORSYTH

John HARRIS

Jack HIGGINS

Robert LUDLUM

Alistair MACLEAN

Wilbur SMITH

James PATTINSON
Crime

John Newton CHANCE

Joyce PORTER

Colin WATSON

Gary PAULSEN
Western

Louis L'AMOUR

T.C. OLSEN

Lilian PEAKE
Romance

Penny JORDAN

Annabel MURRAY

Mervyn PEAKE
Fantasy

C.S. LEWIS

H.P. LOVECRAFT

J.R.R. TOLKIEN

Mary E. PEARCE
Family Stories

Iris BROMIGE

Catherine COOKSON

Monica DICKENS

Pamela OLDFIELD

Diane PEARSON

Miss READ

Sarah SHEARS

Michael PEARCE
Crime

Simon BRETT

Tom KAKONIS

James McCLURE

Iain PEARS
Crime

Gwendoline BUTLER

Jonathan GASH

Jennie MELVILLE

Neville STEED

Diane PEARSON
Historical

Catherine GASKIN

Susan HOWATCH

M.M. KAYE

Mary E. PEARCE

Jean STUBBS

Reay TANNAHILL

Ridley PEARSON
Crime

Jonathan KELLERMAN

Lawrence SANDERS

Margaret PEMBERTON
Historical

Sara HYLTON

Doris MORTMAN

E.V. THOMPSON

Sharon PENMAN
Historical

Morgan LLYWELYN

Neil MUNRO

Edith PARGETER

Nigel TRANTER

John PENN
Crime

W.J. BURLEY

Elizabeth FERRARS

John WAINWRIGHT

Wendy PERRIAM
General

Beryl BAINBRIDGE

Clare BOYLAN

Carol CLEWLOW

Sarah HARRISON

Edna O'BRIEN

Muriel SPARK

Joanna TROLLOPE

Fay WELDON

Thomas PERRY
Adventure

Richard CONDON

Richard COX

Leslie WALLER

Elizabeth PETERS
General

Barbara MICHAELS

Mary STEWART

Patricia WENTWORTH

Phyllis A. WHITNEY

Ellis PETERS
Crime

Sarah CAUDWELL

Michael CLYNES

Lindsey DAVIS

P.C. DOHERTY

Elizabeth EYRE

D.M. GREENWOOD

Ray HARRISON

Tony HILLERMAN

Ellis PETERS (cont.)

William KIENZLE

Peter LOVESEY

K.M. PEYTON
General

Deborah MOGGACH

Bel MOONEY

Beryl KINGSTON

Miss READ

Elvi RHODES

Susan SALLIS

Judith SAXTON

Danielle STEEL

Eileen TOWNSEND

Joanna TROLLOPE

Mary WESLEY

Caryl PHILLIPS
General

William BOYD

Timothy MO

Ben OKRI

Marge PIERCY
General

Marilyn FRENCH

Ursula LE GUIN

Larry McMURTRY

Rosamunde PILCHER
Family Stories

Maeve BINCHY

Barbara Taylor BRADFORD

Iris BROMIGE

Judith GLOVER

Audrey HOWARD

Marie JOSEPH

Richard PITMAN
Crime

Dick FRANCIS

John FRANCOME

Richard RUSSELL

Erin PIZZEY
Family Stories

Maeve BINCHY

Judith SAXTON

Jean PLAIDY
Historical

Valerie ANAND

Evelyn ANTHONY

Dorothy DUNNETT

Pamela HILL

Jane Aiken HODGE

Rosalind LAKER

Norah LOFTS

Diana NORMAN

Edith PARGETER

Anya SETON

Jean STUBBS

Rosemary SUTCLIFF

Nigel TRANTER

Philippa WIAT

Belva PLAIN
Family Stories

Maeve BINCHY

Virginia COFFMAN

Teresa CRANE

Janet DAILEY

Cynthia FREEMAN

Gail GODWIN

Doris MORTMAN

Maisie MOSCO

Lewis ORDE

Claire RAYNER

Anne Rivers SIDDONS

Danielle STEEL

Jessica STIRLING

Rosie THOMAS

Nicola THORNE

Frederik POHL
Science Fiction

Isaac ASIMOV

Greg BEAR

Ray BRADBURY

C.J. CHERRYH

Arthur C. CLARKE

Larry NIVEN

John WYNDHAM

Dudley POPE
Sea

Brian CALLISON

C.S. FORESTER

Alexander FULLERTON

Alexander KENT

Philip McCUTCHAN

Patrick O'BRIAN

Douglas REEMAN

Showell STYLES

John WINGATE

Richard WOODMAN

Joyce PORTER
Crime

Josephine BELL

James PATTINSON

Colin WATSON

Chaim POTOK
General

David GROSSMAN

Amos OZ

Isaac Bashevis SINGER

Anthony POWELL
General

F. Scott FITZGERALD

Graham GREENE

Aldous HUXLEY

Iris MURDOCH

J.B. PRIESTLEY

C.P. SNOW

Evelyn WAUGH

Henry WILLIAMSON

Joe POYER
Adventure

Ian FLEMING

Philip KERR

Amanda PRANTERA
General

J.M. COETZEE

Barry UNSWORTH

Terry PRATCHETT
Fantasy

Douglas ADAMS

Piers ANTHONY

Robert ASPRIN

Terry BROOKS

Alan Dean FOSTER

Harry HARRISON

Dan McGIRT

Grant NAYLOR

Robert RANKIN

Christopher STASHEFF

Anthony PRICE
Adventure

Len DEIGHTON

Clive EGLETON

Colin FORBES

John LE CARRÉ

Helen MACINNES

Julian RATHBONE

Gerald SEYMOUR

Christopher PRIEST
Science Fiction

J.G. BALLARD

Ray BRADBURY

Mary GENTLE

Doris LESSING

Michael MOORCOCK

Keith ROBERTS

John WYNDHAM

J.B. PRIESTLEY
General

Thomas ARMSTRONG

Phyllis BENTLEY

Norman COLLINS

A.J. CRONIN

R.F. DELDERFIELD

John GALSWORTHY

L.P. HARTLEY

Anthony POWELL

C.P. SNOW

Howard SPRING

Angus WILSON

V.S. PRITCHETT
General

John McGAHERN

William TREVOR

Deirdre PURCELL
Family Stories

Maeve BINCHY

Frank DELANEY

Elvi RHODES

Janet TANNER

Mario PUZO
General

Simon BELL

Michael CRICHTON

Barbara PYM
General

A.L. BARKER

Anita BROOKNER

Monica DICKENS

Margaret DRABBLE

Alice Thomas ELLIS

Susan HILL

Mary HOCKING

Elizabeth Jane HOWARD

Molly KEANE

Penelope LIVELY

Shena MACKAY

Elizabeth PALMER

Jean RHYS

Elizabeth TAYLOR

Emma TENNANT

Joanna TROLLOPE

Mary WESLEY

A.N. WILSON

Marjorie QUARTON
Family Stories

Denise ROBERTSON

Susan SALLIS

Sheila RADLEY
Crime

W.J. BURLEY

John HARVEY

Ruth RENDELL

C.F. ROE

Dorothy SIMPSON

June THOMSON

Peter TURNBULL

Robert RANKIN
Science Fiction

Douglas ADAMS

Robert ASPRIN

Terry PRATCHETT

Robert SHECKLEY

Frederic RAPHAEL
General

Howard JACOBSON

Allan MASSIE

John MORTIMER

Piers Paul READ

C.P. SNOW

Julian RATHBONE
Adventure

John GARDNER

Palma HARCOURT

John HARRIS

Robert LUDLUM

Anthony PRICE

Gerald SEYMOUR

Craig THOMAS

Melanie RAWN
Fantasy

Marion Zimmer BRADLEY

David EDDINGS

Anne McCAFFREY

Ernest RAYMOND
General

Ernest HEMINGWAY

Erich Maria REMARQUE

Henry WILLIAMSON

Claire RAYNER
Family Stories

Lucilla ANDREWS

Harry BOWLING

Betty BURTON

Mazo DE LA ROCHE

Helen FORRESTER

Christine Marion FRASER

Winston GRAHAM

Audrey HOWARD

Marie JOSEPH

Lena KENNEDY

Beryl KINGSTON

Anne MELVILLE

Maisie MOSCO

Belva PLAIN

Judith SAXTON

Patricia WENDORF

Miss READ
Family Stories

H.E. BATES

Brenda CLARKE

Monica DICKENS

Jane DUNCAN

Elizabeth GOUDGE

Marie JOSEPH

Mary MELWOOD

Mary E. PEARCE

Rosamunde PILCHER

Susan SALLIS

Sarah SHEARS

D.E. STEVENSON

Angela THIRKELL

Piers Paul READ
General

Kingsley AMIS

Paul BAILEY

Graham GREENE

Allan MASSIE

Ian McEWAN

Frederic RAPHAEL

Paul THEROUX

Angus WILSON

Tom REAMY
Fantasy

Ray BRADBURY

Richard MATHESON

Douglas REEMAN
Sea

Ronald BASSETT

Brian CALLISON

Bernard CORNWELL

Clive CUSSLER

C.S. FORESTER

John HARRIS

Max HENNESSY

Geoffrey JENKINS

Alexander KENT

Philip McCUTCHAN

Nicholas MONSARRAT

Patrick O'BRIAN

Dudley POPE

Douglas SCOTT

Antony TREW

John WINGATE

John WINTON

Erich Maria REMARQUE
General

Ernest HEMINGWAY

Ernest RAYMOND

Paul WATKINS

William WHARTON

Henry WILLIAMSON

Mary RENAULT
General

Gillian BRADSHAW

Dorothy DUNNETT

Robert GRAVES

Allan MASSIE

Rosemary SUTCLIFF

Gore VIDAL

Ruth RENDELL
Crime

Liza CODY

Patricia D. CORNWELL

Colin DEXTER

Frances FYFIELD

Elizabeth GEORGE

Lesley GRANT-ADAMSON

S.T. HAYMON

Patricia HIGHSMITH

P.D. JAMES

Sheila RADLEY

Dorothy SIMPSON

Barbara VINE

Margaret YORKE

Elvi RHODES
Family Stories

Maeve BINCHY

Emma BLAIR

Elizabeth CADELL

Catherine COOKSON

Helen FORRESTER

Christine Marion FRASER

Iris GOWER

Marie JOSEPH

Beryl KINGSTON

Elisabeth McNEILL

Rosamunde PILCHER

Deirdre PURCELL

Susan SALLIS

Jean RHYS
General

Margaret DRABBLE

Barbara PYM

Mary WESLEY

Anne RICE
Supernatural

Nancy COLLINS

Stephen KING

George R. MARTIN

Dan SIMMONS

Philip RICKMAN
Supernatural

Steve HARRIS

James HERBERT

Judith M. RILEY
Historical

Diana NORMAN

Edith PARGETER

Alexandra RIPLEY
Historical

Margaret MITCHELL

Frank YERBY

Mike RIPLEY
Crime

Simon BRETT

John HARVEY

Susan MOODY

Mark TIMLIN

Harold ROBBINS
The 'Smart Set'

Sally BEAUMAN

Pat BOOTH

Celia BRAYFIELD

Sandra BROWN

Julie BURCHILL

Jackie COLLINS

Joan COLLINS

Shirley CONRAN

Jilly COOPER

Elizabeth GAGE

Burt HIRSCHFELD

Judith KRANTZ

Caryl RIVERS

Jacqueline SUSANN

Barbara TRAPIDO

Ann Victoria ROBERTS
Family Stories

Marie JOSEPH

Beryl KINGSTON

Keith ROBERTS
Fantasy

Robert HOLDSTOCK

Christopher PRIEST

Denise ROBERTSON
Family Stories

Tessa BARCLAY
Emma BLAIR
Marjorie QUARTON
Susan SALLIS
Barbara VICTOR

Denise ROBINS
Romance

Lucilla ANDREWS
Barbara CARTLAND
Marion CHESNEY
Patricia ROBINS
Elizabeth SEIFERT

Patricia ROBINS
Romance

Lucilla ANDREWS
Marion CHESNEY
Denise ROBINS
Elizabeth SEIFERT
Sheila WALSH

Derek ROBINSON
War

Larry FORRESTER
W.E.B. GRIFFIN
John HARRIS
Max HENNESSY
Hammond INNES
Paul WATKINS

C.F. ROE
Crime

Josephine BELL
Ann GRANGER
Janet LAURENCE
Sheila RADLEY
Dorothy SIMPSON

Jane ROGERS
General

A.S. BYATT
Sally EMERSON
Jane GARDAM
Alison LURIE
Candia McWILLIAM

Annette ROOME
Crime

Sarah CAUDWELL
Frances FYFIELD
Janet LAURENCE
John SHERWOOD
Dorothy SIMPSON

Jonathan ROSS
Crime

W.J. BURLEY

John CREASEY

Reginald HILL

Janet NEEL

Michael UNDERWOOD

R.D. WINGFIELD

Judith ROSSNER
General

Lisa ALTHER

Marilyn FRENCH

Toni MORRISON

Ann OAKLEY

Anne TYLER

Philip ROTH
General

Saul BELLOW

Joseph HELLER

Jay McINERNEY

Bernard MALAMUD

Bernice RUBENS

Leslie THOMAS

John UPDIKE

Kenneth ROYCE
Adventure

Jon CLEARY

Len DEIGHTON

Lawrence SANDERS

Bernice RUBENS
General

Patricia ANGADI

Beryl BAINBRIDGE

Anita BROOKNER

Margaret DRABBLE

Alice Thomas ELLIS

Iris MURDOCH

Philip ROTH

Muriel SPARK

Paul THEROUX

A.N. WILSON

Rudy RUCKER
Science Fiction

Philip K. DICK

K.W. JETER

Salman RUSHDIE
General

Anthony BURGESS

Angela CARTER

John FOWLES

Alasdair GRAY

Salman RUSHDIE (cont.)

Gabriel Garcia MARQUEZ

Gita MEHTA

Michael ONDAATJE

Vikram SETH

Antony SHER

Joanna RUSS
Science Fiction

Samuel R. DELANY

Ursula LE GUIN

Eric Frank RUSSELL
Science Fiction

Arthur C. CLARKE

Stanislaw LEM

Martin RUSSELL
Crime

Dick FRANCIS

Mary McMULLEN

Margaret YORKE

Richard RUSSELL
Crime

Dick FRANCIS

Paul MYERS

Richard PITMAN

Douglas RUTHERFORD
Crime

Simon BRETT

Jon CLEARY

Mark DANIEL

Dick FRANCIS

John FRANCOME

Bob JUDD

Fred SABERHAGEN
Science Fiction

Poul ANDERSON

Isaac ASIMOV

Julian MAY

Robert SILVERBERG

Ian ST. JAMES
Adventure

Gavin ESLER

Gerald SEYMOUR

Nicholas SALAMAN
Humour

Roddy DOYLE

Tom SHARPE

J.D. SALINGER
General

Truman CAPOTE

Geoff DYER

Barry HINES

Carson McCULLERS

Flannery O'CONNOR

Carola SALISBURY
Historical

Victoria HOLT

Sara HYLTON

Susan SALLIS
Family Stories

Tessa BARCLAY

Iris BROMIGE

Elizabeth CADELL

Josephine COX

Lena KENNEDY

Beryl KINGSTON

Pamela OLDFIELD

Rosamunde PILCHER

Marjorie QUARTON

Miss READ

Elvi RHODES

Denise ROBERTSON

Sarah SHEARS

Lawrence SANDERS
Adventure

Robin COOK

Ken FOLLETT

Jonathan KELLERMAN

Duncan KYLE

Robert LUDLUM

Ridley PEARSON

Kenneth ROYCE

Sidney SHELDON

Richard STARK

John TRENHAILE

John SANDFORD
Crime

William BAYER

James Lee BURKE

Thomas HARRIS

David L. LINDSEY

John SAUL
Supernatural

Graham MASTERTON

Dennis WHEATLEY

Alan SAVAGE
Adventure

James CLAVELL

Robert ELEGANT

David MORRELL

Alan SAVAGE (cont.)

Marc OLDEN

Eric VAN LUSTBADER

Julian Jay SAVARIN
Adventure

Campbell ARMSTRONG

John LE CARRÉ

Craig THOMAS

Judith SAXTON
Family Stories

Harry BOWLING

Barbara Taylor BRADFORD

Teresa CRANE

Janet DAILEY

Helen FORRESTER

Judith GLOVER

Beryl KINGSTON

Pamela OLDFIELD

Rosamunde PILCHER

Erin PIZZEY

Claire RAYNER

Danielle STEEL

Janet TANNER

Nicola THORNE

Judy TURNER

Paul SAYER
General

David COOK

Ken KESEY

Dorothy L. SAYERS
Crime

Margery ALLINGHAM

Josephine BELL

John Dickson CARR

Agatha CHRISTIE

Georgette HEYER

Michael INNES

P.D. JAMES

Ngaio MARSH

Rex STOUT

Josephine TEY

Patricia WENTWORTH

Jack SCHAEFER
Western

Louis L'AMOUR

Bill WADE

Douglas SCOTT
Sea

Brian CALLISON

Eric J. COLLENETTE

Alan EVANS

Alexander FULLERTON

John HARRIS

Max HENNESSY

Jack HIGGINS

A.E. LANGSFORD

Douglas REEMAN

Peter TONKIN

John WINTON

Paul SCOTT
General

Nadine GORDIMER

Graham GREENE

Ruth Prawer JHABVALA

Doris LESSING

Olivia MANNING

John MASTERS

Tim SEBASTIAN
Adventure

Ted ALLBEURY

Len DEIGHTON

Gavin ESLER

John LE CARRÉ

Gerald SEYMOUR

Elizabeth SEIFERT
Romance

Lucilla ANDREWS

Anne MATHER

Denise ROBINS

Patricia ROBINS

Sheila WALSH

Owen SELA
Adventure

Adam HALL

Robert LITTELL

Christopher SHERLOCK

Vikram SETH
General

Anthony BURGESS

Amit CHAUDHURI

James A. MICHENER

V.S. NAIPAUL

R.K. NARAYAN

Salman RUSHDIE

Anya SETON
Historical

Pamela BELLE

Madeleine BRENT

Elizabeth BYRD

Daphne DU MAURIER

Dorothy DUNNETT

Dorothy EDEN

Elizabeth GOUDGE

Winston GRAHAM

Anya SETON (cont.)

Cynthia HARROD-EAGLES
Jane Aiken HODGE
Victoria HOLT
Norah LOFTS
Jean PLAIDY
Mary STEWART
Jean STUBBS
Rosemary SUTCLIFF

Gerald SEYMOUR
Adventure

Ted ALLBEURY
Evelyn ANTHONY
Jeffrey ARCHER
Desmond BAGLEY
Tom CLANCY
Clive CUSSLER
Len DEIGHTON
Gavin ESLER
Colin FORBES
Frederick FORSYTH
Jack HIGGINS
John LE CARRÉ
Robert LUDLUM
Gavin LYALL
Helen MACINNES
Anthony PRICE
Julian RATHBONE
Ian ST. JAMES
Tim SEBASTIAN
Terence STRONG
Craig THOMAS
John TRENHAILE

Dell SHANNON
Crime

Lesley EGAN
Erle Stanley GARDNER
Ed McBAIN
T. Jefferson PARKER
Sara WOODS

Margery SHARP
General

Beryl BAINBRIDGE
Monica DICKENS
Margaret DRABBLE
Muriel SPARK

Tom SHARPE
Humour

Kingsley AMIS
Guy BELLAMY
Malcolm BRADBURY
Roy CLARKE
J.P. DONLEAVY
George Macdonald FRASER
Howard JACOBSON
David LODGE

David NOBBS

Nicholas SALAMAN

Leslie THOMAS

Peter TINNISWOOD

Keith WATERHOUSE

Bob SHAW
Science Fiction

Douglas ADAMS

Isaac ASIMOV

Greg BEAR

C. J. CHERRYH

Arthur C. CLARKE

James P. HOGAN

Stanislaw LEM

Michael MOORCOCK

Robert SHECKLEY

Irwin SHAW
General

Graham GREENE

Arthur HAILEY

John IRVING

Wilbur SMITH

Howard SPRING

John STEINBECK

John UPDIKE

Herman WOUK

Simon SHAW
Crime

Marian BABSON

Anthea COHEN

Patricia HIGHSMITH

Sarah SHEARS
Family Stories

Lyn ANDREWS

Josephine COX

Jane DUNCAN

Helen FORRESTER

Christine Marion FRASER

Sara FRASER

Elisabeth McNEILL

Anne MELVILLE

Frances PAIGE

Mary E. PEARCE

Miss READ

Susan SALLIS

Mary Jane STAPLES

Robert SHECKLEY
Science Fiction

Douglas ADAMS

Robert RANKIN

Bob SHAW

Sidney SHELDON
Adventure

Elizabeth ADLER

Jeffrey ARCHER

Richard CONDON

Nelson DE MILLE

Clive EGLETON

Arthur HAILEY

Thomas HARRIS

Robert LUDLUM

Lawrence SANDERS

Wilbur SMITH

Jacqueline SUSANN

Antony SHER
General

Michael ONDAATJE

Salman RUSHDIE

Christopher SHERLOCK
Adventure

Robert LITTELL

Owen SELA

Don SILVERMAN

Wilbur SMITH

Richard STARK

John SHERWOOD
Crime

Douglas CLARK

Michael GILBERT

Susan KELLY

Janet LAWRENCE

Gladys MITCHELL

Gwen MOFFAT

Annette ROOME

STAYNES & STOREY

Carol SHIELDS
General

Margaret ATWOOD

Susan HILL

Alison LURIE

Anita SHREVE
Crime

Mary Higgins CLARK

Judith KELMAN

Nevil SHUTE
Adventure

Desmond BAGLEY

H.E. BATES

Victor CANNING

Jon CLEARY

Paul GALLICO

Hammond INNES

Geoffrey JENKINS

James LEASOR

John MASTERS

Nicholas MONSARRAT

Frank G. SLAUGHTER

Nigel TRANTER

Elleston TREVOR

Morris WEST

Anne Rivers SIDDONS
Family Stories

Lewis ORDE

Belva PLAIN

Rosie THOMAS

Barbara VICTOR

Alan SILLITOE
General

Kingsley AMIS

Stan BARSTOW

Malcolm BRADBURY

John BRAINE

D.H. LAWRENCE

David LODGE

Stanley MIDDLETON

David NOBBS

David STOREY

John UPDIKE

Robert SILVERBERG
Science Fiction

Poul ANDERSON

Ray BRADBURY

Gordon R. DICKSON

Ursula LE GUIN

Julian MAY

Michael MOORCOCK

Fred SABERHAGEN

Don SILVERMAN
Adventure

David MORRELL

Christopher SHERLOCK

Richard STARK

Eric VAN LUSTBADER

Clifford D. SIMAK
Science Fiction

Isaac ASIMOV

Ray BRADBURY

Richard COWPER

Gordon R. DICKSON

John WYNDHAM

Georges SIMENON
Crime

Raymond CHANDLER

Agatha CHRISTIE

John CREASEY

Georges SIMENON (cont.)

Nicolas FREELING

Mark HEBDEN

H.R.F. KEATING

Philip KERR

Dan SIMMONS
Fantasy

Ray BRADBURY

Nancy COLLINS

Stephen KING

Dean R. KOONTZ

Anne RICE

Dorothy SIMPSON
Crime

Sarah CAUDWELL

Agatha CHRISTIE

Elizabeth FERRARS

Georgette HEYER

Ngaio MARSH

Janet NEEL

Sheila RADLEY

Ruth RENDELL

C.F. ROE

Annette ROOME

STAYNES & STOREY

Isaac Bashevis SINGER
General

Chinua ACHEBE

Saul BELLOW

Angela CARTER

David GROSSMAN

Primo LEVI

Bernard MALAMUD

Amos OZ

Chaim POTOK

June Flaum SINGER
The 'Smart Set'

Freda BRIGHT

Jacqueline BRISKIN

Sandra BROWN

Jilly COOPER

Julie ELLIS

Elizabeth GAGE

Thomas TRYON

Frank G. SLAUGHTER
General

Vernon COLEMAN

Robin COOK

A.J. CRONIN

Henry DENKER

Arthur HAILEY

Nevil SHUTE

Frank YERBY

Jane SMILEY
General

E.L. DOCTOROW

John UPDIKE

Clark Ashton SMITH
Fantasy

August DERLETH

H.P. LOVECRAFT

Guy N. SMITH
Supernatural

James HERBERT

Richard LAYMON

Iain Crichton SMITH
General

George Mackay BROWN

Robin JENKINS

Joan SMITH
Crime

Margery ALLINGHAM

Sarah CAUDWELL

Sara PARETSKY

Wilbur SMITH
Adventure

Eric AMBLER

Desmond BAGLEY

James CLAVELL

Jon CLEARY

Ken FOLLETT

Arthur HAILEY

Jack HIGGINS

Hammond INNES

Geoffrey JENKINS

Gavin LYALL

Alistair MACLEAN

James A. MICHENER

Alan PATON

Harry PATTERSON

Irwin SHAW

Sidney SHELDON

Christopher SHERLOCK

Elleston TREVOR

Leon URIS

C.P. SNOW
General

Anthony BURGESS

William COOPER

Lawrence DURRELL

E.M. FORSTER

Graham GREENE

L.P. HARTLEY

Pamela Hansford JOHNSON

C.P. SNOW (cont.)

Thomas KENEALLY
Anthony POWELL
J.B. PRIESTLEY
Frederic RAPHAEL
J.I.M. STEWART
Evelyn WAUGH
Angus WILSON
Bernice RUBENS
Margery SHARP
Elizabeth TAYLOR
Rose TREMAIN
William TREVOR
Evelyn WAUGH
Fay WELDON
A.N. WILSON

Muriel SPARK
General

Margaret ATWOOD
Beryl BAINBRIDGE
Lynne Reid BANKS
Nina BAWDEN
Brigid BROPHY
Isabel COLEGATE
Barbara COMYNS
Margaret DRABBLE
Alice Thomas ELLIS
Margaret FORSTER
Jane GARDAM
Susan HILL
Elizabeth Jane HOWARD
Henry JAMES
Pamela Hansford JOHNSON
Doris LESSING
Penelope LIVELY
Penelope MORTIMER
Iris MURDOCH
Wendy PERRIAM

Mickey SPILLANE
Crime

James M. CAIN
Raymond CHANDLER
James Hadley CHASE
Robert FERRIGNO

Howard SPRING
General

Thomas ARMSTRONG
Stan BARSTOW
H.E. BATES
Phyllis BENTLEY
Taylor CALDWELL
Alexander CORDELL
A.J. CRONIN
R.F. DELDERFIELD
Monica DICKENS
E.M. FORSTER
Winston GRAHAM
L.P. HARTLEY

Winifred HOLTBY

Richard LLEWELLYN

W. Somerset MAUGHAM

J.B. PRIESTLEY

Irwin SHAW

Elizabeth TAYLOR

Henry WILLIAMSON

Brian STABLEFORD
Science Fiction

Brian W. ALDISS

Isaac ASIMOV

Diana STAINFORTH
Family Stories

Janet DAILEY

Suzanne GOODWIN

Margaret GRAHAM

Rosie THOMAS

Mary STANTON
Fantasy

Robert ADAMS

Stephen LAWS

Mary Jane STAPLES
Family Stories

Harry BOWLING

Marie JOSEPH

Lena KENNEDY

Sarah SHEARS

Richard STARK
Adventure

David MORRELL

Lawrence SANDERS

Christopher SHERLOCK

Don SILVERMAN

Douglas TERMAN

Christopher STASHEFF
Fantasy

Robert ASPRIN

Anne McCAFFREY

Dan McGIRT

Terry PRATCHETT

STAYNES & STOREY
Crime

Antonia FRASER

S.T. HAYMON

John SHERWOOD

Dorothy SIMPSON

Neville STEED
Crime

Marian BABSON

Jonathan GASH

Iain PEARS

Audrie MANLEY-TUCKER

Anne MATHER

Carole MORTIMER

Betty NEELS

Kay THORPE

Danielle STEEL
Family Stories

Charlotte Vale ALLEN

Barbara Taylor BRADFORD

Janet DAILEY

Cynthia FREEMAN

Rona JAFFE

Claire LORRIMER

Colleen McCULLOUGH

Una-Mary PARKER

Rosamunde PILCHER

Belva PLAIN

Judith SAXTON

Nicola THORNE

Helen VAN SLYKE

Jessica STEELE
Romance

Charlotte Vale ALLEN

Joyce DINGWELL

Jane DONNELLY

Catherine GEORGE

Penny JORDAN

Charlotte LAMB

Marguerite STEEN
General

Thomas ARMSTRONG

Taylor CALDWELL

Joyce CARY

Ivy COMPTON-BURNETT

Dorothy EDEN

Norah LOFTS

Colleen McCULLOUGH

Joy PACKER

John STEINBECK
General

Erskine CALDWELL

William FAULKNER

F. Scott FITZGERALD

Ernest HEMINGWAY

Harper LEE

Norman MAILER

Alan PATON

Irwin SHAW

William STYRON

John UPDIKE

David STEPHEN
General

Henry WILLIAMSON

Miss READ

Essie SUMMERS

Elswyth THANE

Angela THIRKELL

Kay STEPHENS
Family Stories

Brenda CLARKE

Brenda JAGGER

Bruce STERLING
Science Fiction

John BRUNNER

William GIBSON

Anne STEVENSON
Romance

Dorothy EDEN

Phyllis A. WHITNEY

D.E. STEVENSON
Family Stories

Lucilla ANDREWS

Iris BROMIGE

Elizabeth CADELL

Catherine COOKSON

Mazo DE LA ROCHE

Monica DICKENS

Jane DUNCAN

Mary MELWOOD

J.I.M. STEWART
General

William COOPER

C.P. SNOW

Mary STEWART
General

Joan AIKEN

Madeleine BRENT

Virginia COFFMAN

Daphne DU MAURIER

Dorothy DUNNETT

Dorothy EDEN

Clare FRANCIS

Catherine GASKIN

Jane Aiken HODGE

Victoria HOLT

M.M. KAYE

Caroline LLEWELLYN

Helen MACINNES

Barbara MICHAELS

Joy PACKER

Elizabeth PETERS

Anya SETON

Mary STEWART (cont.)

Rosemary SUTCLIFF

Phyllis A. WHITNEY

Caroline STICKLAND
Family Stories

Charles GIDLEY

Malcolm MACDONALD

Jessica STIRLING
Family Stories

Tessa BARCLAY

Emma BLAIR

Virginia COFFMAN

Doris DAVIDSON

Margaret Thomson DAVIS

Mazo DE LA ROCHE

Christine Marion FRASER

Winston GRAHAM

Victoria HOLT

Audrey HOWARD

Brenda JAGGER

Anne MELVILLE

Mary MINTON

Connie MONK

Catrin MORGAN

Belva PLAIN

Reay TANNAHILL

E.V. THOMPSON

Jan WEBSTER

David STOREY
General

Stan BARSTOW

Malcolm BRADBURY

Mervyn JONES

James KELMAN

D.H. LAWRENCE

Stanley MIDDLETON

Alan SILLITOE

John UPDIKE

Rex STOUT
Crime

Robert CAMPBELL

John Dickson CARR

Raymond CHANDLER

James Hadley CHASE

Freeman Wills CROFTS

Erle Stanley GARDNER

Robert GOLDSBOROUGH

Dorothy L. SAYERS

Peter STRAUB
Supernatural

Jonathan AYCLIFFE

Stephen KING

Dean R. KOONTZ

Whitley STRIEBER
Crime

Jonathan KELLERMAN

Dean R. KOONTZ

Terence STRONG
War

W.E.B. GRIFFIN

Gavin LYALL

Gerald SEYMOUR

L.K. TRUSCOTT

Vivian STUART
Historical

Charles GIDLEY

Cynthia HARROD-EAGLES

Colleen McCULLOUGH

Malcolm MACDONALD

E.V. THOMPSON

Jean STUBBS
General

D.K. BROSTER

Elizabeth BYRD

Catherine COOKSON

Winston GRAHAM

Susan HOWATCH

Diane PEARSON

Jean PLAIDY

Anya SETON

Reay TANNAHILL

E.V. THOMPSON

Showell STYLES
Sea

C.S. FORESTER

Patrick O'BRIAN

Dudley POPE

Richard WOODMAN

William STYRON
General

Saul BELLOW

Ralph ELLISON

William FAULKNER

Richard FORD

Ernest HEMINGWAY

Norman MAILER

John STEINBECK

John UPDIKE

Alice WALKER

Richard WRIGHT

Essie SUMMERS
Family Stories

Elizabeth CADELL

Mary MELWOOD

D.E. STEVENSON

Margaret SUNLEY
Family Stories

Janet DAILEY

Beryl KINGSTON

Jacqueline SUSANN
The 'Smart Set'

Sally BEAUMAN

Sandra BROWN

Burt HIRSCHFELD

Harold ROBBINS

Rosemary SUTCLIFF
Historical

Morgan LLYWELYN

Allan MASSIE

Diana NORMAN

Edith PARGETER

Jean PLAIDY

Mary RENAULT

Anya SETON

Mary STEWART

Victor SUTHREN
Sea

C.S. FORESTER

Alexander KENT

Patrick O'BRIAN

Graham SWIFT
General

Peter ACKROYD

Julian BARNES

John FOWLES

Ian McEWAN

Julian SYMONS
Crime

John Dickson CARR

Agatha CHRISTIE

Ray HARRISON

Patricia HIGHSMITH

Peter LOVESEY

Amy MYERS

Reay TANNAHILL
Family Stories

Tessa BARCLAY

Margaret Thomson DAVIS

Dorothy DUNNETT

Zoe FAIRBAIRNS

Susan HOWATCH

Beryl KINGSTON

Diane PEARSON

Jessica STIRLING

Jean STUBBS

Janet TANNER
Family Stories

Noel BARBER

Maeve BINCHY

Barbara Taylor BRADFORD

Catherine COOKSON

Janet DAILEY

Sara FRASER

Iris GOWER

Hilda McKENZIE

Pamela OLDFIELD

Deirdre PURCELL

Judith SAXTON

Elizabeth TAYLOR
General

Monica DICKENS

Margaret DRABBLE

Elizabeth Jane HOWARD

Rosamond LEHMANN

Olivia MANNING

Elizabeth PALMER

Barbara PYM

Muriel SPARK

Howard SPRING

Peter TAYLOR
General

William FAULKNER

Angus WILSON

Emma TENNANT
General

A.L. BARKER

Penelope FITZGERALD

Iris MURDOCH

Barbara PYM

Fay WELDON

Sheri S. TEPPER
Science Fiction

Ursula LE GUIN

Anne McCAFFREY

Andre NORTON

Douglas TERMAN
Adventure

Tom CLANCY

David MORRELL

Richard STARK

Josephine TEY
Crime

Margery ALLINGHAM

John Dickson CARR

Agatha CHRISTIE

Edmund CRISPIN

Freeman Wills CROFTS

Michael INNES

Dorothy L. SAYERS

Elswyth THANE
Romance

Iris BROMIGE

Elizabeth CADELL

Elizabeth GOUDGE

D.E. STEVENSON

Paul THEROUX
General

Saul BELLOW

William BOYD

Anthony BURGESS

Graham GREENE

Ernest HEMINGWAY

Brian MOORE

V.S. NAIPAUL

Piers Paul READ

Bernice RUBENS

Colin THUBRON

John UPDIKE

Angela THIRKELL
General

E.F. BENSON

Lettice COOPER

Mary MELWOOD

Miss READ

D.E. STEVENSON

Christine THOMAS
Family Stories

Harry BOWLING

Lena KENNEDY

Craig THOMAS
Adventure

Campbell ARMSTRONG

Desmond BAGLEY

Tom CLANCY

Clive CUSSLER

Nelson DE MILLE

James FOLLETT

Ken FOLLETT

Colin FORBES

Frederick FORSYTH

Palma HARCOURT

Jack HIGGINS

Gavin LYALL

Julian RATHBONE

Julian Jay SAVARIN

Gerald SEYMOUR

John TRENHAILE

D.M. THOMAS
General

Julian BARNES

John FOWLES

Brian MOORE

Virginia WOOLF

Elizabeth M. THOMAS
Fantasy

Jean M. AUEL

Nicholas LUARD

Leslie THOMAS
General

Kingsley AMIS

Malcolm BRADBURY

John BRAINE

George Macdonald FRASER

Richard GORDON

Joseph HELLER

David LODGE

David NOBBS

Philip ROTH

Tom SHARPE

Peter TINNISWOOD

John UPDIKE

Keith WATERHOUSE

Donald WESTLAKE

Rosie THOMAS
Family Stories

Hilda McKENZIE

Maisie MOSCO

Lewis ORDE

Belva PLAIN

Anne Rivers SIDDONS

Diana STAINFORTH

Nicola THORNE

Dee WILLIAMS

Ross THOMAS
Crime

James M. CAIN

Dashiell HAMMETT

Ross MACDONALD

Leslie WALLER

E.V. THOMPSON
Historical

Philip BOAST

Alexander CORDELL

R.F. DELDERFIELD

Daphne DU MAURIER

Catherine GASKIN

Winston GRAHAM

Cynthia HARROD-EAGLES

Susan HOWATCH

Beryl KINGSTON

Rosalind LAKER

Malcolm MACDONALD

Margaret PEMBERTON

Jessica STIRLING

Vivian STUART

Jean STUBBS

Patricia WENDORF

Sarah WOODHOUSE

Grace THOMPSON
Family Stories

Catherine COOKSON

Iris GOWER

Judy TURNER

Margaret Thomson DAVIS

Evelyn HOOD

Beryl KINGSTON

Elizabeth MURPHY

Pamela OLDFIELD

Belva PLAIN

Judith SAXTON

Danielle STEEL

Rosie THOMAS

Jim THOMPSON
Crime

James M. CAIN

James ELLROY

Charles WILLEFORD

June THOMSON
Crime

W.J. BURLEY

Agatha CHRISTIE

Douglas CLARK

Elizabeth FERRARS

P.D. JAMES

Ngaio MARSH

Sheila RADLEY

Patricia WENTWORTH

Nicola THORNE
Family Stories

Charlotte Vale ALLEN

Tessa BARCLAY

Emma BLAIR

Barbara Taylor BRADFORD

Kay THORPE
Romance

Charlotte LAMB

Judith McNAUGHT

Anne MATHER

Carole MORTIMER

Jessica STEELE

Colin THUBRON
General

Ian McEWAN

Paul THEROUX

Jeanette WINTERSON

Mark TIMLIN
Crime

Simon BRETT

Mike RIPLEY

Gillian TINDALL
General

Rachel BILLINGTON

Anita BROOKNER

Margaret DRABBLE

Rosemary FRIEDMAN

Penelope LIVELY

Deborah MOGGACH

Peter TINNISWOOD
Humour

Kingsley AMIS

H.E. BATES

Guy BELLAMY

Roy CLARKE

George Macdonald FRASER

David NOBBS

Tom SHARPE

Leslie THOMAS

Keith WATERHOUSE

P.G. WODEHOUSE

J.R.R. TOLKIEN
Fantasy

Terry BROOKS

Hugh COOK

Stephen DONALDSON

David EDDINGS

Guy Gavriel KAY

C.S. LEWIS

Mervyn PEAKE

Michael TOLKIN
Crime

Robert BARNARD

Patricia HIGHSMITH

Peter TONKIN
Sea

Eric J. COLLENETTE

Alan EVANS

Alexander KENT

Philip McCUTCHAN

Douglas SCOTT

Eileen TOWNSEND
Family Stories

John Gordon DAVIS

R.F. DELDERFIELD

Colleen McCULLOUGH

Rosamunde PILCHER

Judy TURNER

Sue TOWNSEND
Humour

Clare BOYLAN

Roy CLARKE

Keith WATERHOUSE

Nigel TRANTER
Historical

D.K. BROSTER

Bernard CORNWELL

Dorothy DUNNETT

Winston GRAHAM

Sharon PENMAN

Jean PLAIDY

Nevil SHUTE

Barbara TRAPIDO
The 'Smart Set'

Jacqueline BRISKIN

Jilly COOPER

Harold ROBBINS

Rose TREMAIN
General

A.S. BYATT

Muriel SPARK

Mary WESLEY

John TRENHAILE
Adventure

Jeffrey ARCHER

Campbell ARMSTRONG

Nelson DE MILLE

Daniel EASTERMAN

James FOLLETT

Colin FORBES

Frederick FORSYTH

John GARDNER

John LE CARRÉ

Lawrence SANDERS

Gerald SEYMOUR

Craig THOMAS

Elleston TREVOR
Adventure

Frederick FORSYTH

Nicholas GUILD

Adam HALL

Jack HIGGINS

Hammond INNES

John MASTERS

J.K. MAYO

Nevil SHUTE

Wilbur SMITH

William TREVOR
General

Anita BROOKNER

Jane GARDAM

Graham GREENE

Susan HILL

Jennifer JOHNSTON

James JOYCE

Molly KEANE

John McGAHERN

Stanley MIDDLETON

Brian MOORE

Edna O'BRIEN

V.S. PRITCHETT

Muriel SPARK

Antony TREW
Sea

Ronald BASSETT

Brian CALLISON

Hammond INNES

Sam LLEWELLYN

Philip McCUTCHAN

Douglas REEMAN

John WINGATE

Joanna TROLLOPE
General

Nina BAWDEN

Anita BROOKNER

Isabel COLEGATE

Barbara COMYNS

Margaret DRABBLE

Daphne DU MAURIER

Margaret FORSTER

Georgina HAMMICK

Susan HOWATCH

Wendy PERRIAM

Rosamunde PILCHER

Barbara PYM

Mary WESLEY

Antonia WHITE

M.J. TROW
Crime

W.J. BURLEY

Ray HARRISON

Amy MYERS

L.K. TRUSCOTT
War

W.E.B. GRIFFIN

Terence STRONG

Thomas TRYON
The 'Smart Set'

Celia BRAYFIELD

Shirley CONRAN

Judith KRANTZ

June Flaum SINGER

Peter TURNBULL
Crime

S.T. HAYMON

Bill KNOX

Ed McBAIN

Sheila RADLEY

John WAINWRIGHT

Judy TURNER
Family Stories

Lewis ORDE

Judith SAXTON

Grace THOMPSON

Eileen TOWNSEND

Barbara VICTOR

Scott TUROW
Crime

Philip FRIEDMAN

Frances FYFIELD

John GRISHAM

Steve MARTINI

Anne TYLER
General

Lisa ALTHER

Margaret ATWOOD

Lynne Reid BANKS

Pat BARKER

Ethan CANIN

Louise ERDRICH

Richard FORD

Marilyn FRENCH

Suzanne GOODWIN

Alice HOFFMAN

Alison LURIE

Bobbie Ann MASON

Sue MILLER

Lorrie MOORE

Alice MUNRO

Judith ROSSNER

Mary WESLEY

Michael UNDERWOOD
Crime

Robert BARNARD

Gwendoline BUTLER

Sarah CAUDWELL

Michael GILBERT

Gerald HAMMOND

H.R.F. KEATING

Peter LOVESEY

Janet NEEL

Roger ORMEROD

Jonathan ROSS

John WAINWRIGHT

Patricia WENTWORTH

Ted WOOD

Sara WOODS

Barry UNSWORTH
General

Peter ACKROYD

John BANVILLE

Bruce CHATWIN

J.M. COETZEE

John FOWLES

William GOLDING

Stephen GREGORY
Thomas KENEALLY
Brian MOORE
Robert NYE
Amanda PRANTERA
William STYRON
Paul THEROUX
Leslie THOMAS
Gore VIDAL

John UPDIKE
General

Martin AMIS
Saul BELLOW
Anthony BURGESS
John CHEEVER
E.L. DOCTOROW
Lawrence DURRELL
Richard FORD
David GATES
Joseph HELLER
John IRVING
Ken KESEY
Larry McMURTRY
Norman MAILER
Vladimir NABOKOV
John O'HARA
Philip ROTH
Irwin SHAW
Alan SILLITOE
Jane SMILEY
John STEINBECK
David STOREY

Leon URIS
General

Saul BELLOW
Howard FAST
James A. MICHENER
Wilbur SMITH
Morris WEST

Andrew VACHSS
Crime

James M. CAIN
Eugene IZZI
Joseph KOENIG
Charles WILLEFORD

Denys VAL BAKER
General

H.E. BATES
Vernon COLEMAN
Daphne DU MAURIER
Winston GRAHAM

Jack VANCE
Science Fiction

Frank HERBERT

Michael MOORCOCK

David WINGROVE

Eric VAN LUSTBADER
Adventure

Martin BOOTH

Robert CARTER

James CLAVELL

Robert ELEGANT

Michael HARTLAND

Robert LUDLUM

David MORRELL

Marc OLDEN

Alan SAVAGE

Don SILVERMAN

Helen VAN SLYKE
Family Stories

Charlotte Vale ALLEN

Virginia COFFMAN

Janet DAILEY

Cynthia FREEMAN

Gail GODWIN

Danielle STEEL

Barbara VICTOR

Barbara VICTOR
Family Stories

Denise ROBERTSON

Anne Rivers SIDDONS

Judy TURNER

Helen VAN SLYKE

Dee WILLIAMS

Gore VIDAL
Historical

Gillian BRADSHAW

John CHEEVER

Robert GRAVES

Allan MASSIE

James A. MICHENER

Mary RENAULT

John UPDIKE

Tom WOLFE

Elizabeth VILLARS
Family Stories

Barbara Taylor BRADFORD

Brenda JAGGER

Penny JORDAN

Janet TANNER

Penny VINCENZI
The 'Smart Set'

Celia BRAYFIELD

Shirley CONRAN

Jackie COLLINS

Lynda LA PLANTE

Barbara VINE
Crime

Frances HEGARTY

Patricia HIGHSMITH

P.D. JAMES

Ruth RENDELL

Bill WADE
Western

Matt CHISHOLM

Louis L'AMOUR

Jack SCHAEFER

John WAGNER
Fantasy

Clive BARKER

Jamie DELANO

Neil GAIMAN

Frank MILLER

Alan MOORE

John WAINWRIGHT
Crime

Jeffrey ASHFORD

Gerald HAMMOND

Mark HEBDEN

Reginald HILL

Alan HUNTER

Roderic JEFFRIES

H.R.F. KEATING

Bill KNOX

John PENN

Peter TURNBULL

Michael UNDERWOOD

Eric WRIGHT

Alice WALKER
General

James BALDWIN

Ellen DOUGLAS

Rose GUY

Marsha HUNT

Terry McMILLAN

Toni MORRISON

Gloria NAYLOR

William STYRON

Leslie WALLER
Adventure

Richard CONDON

Richard COX

Arthur HAILEY

Thomas PERRY

Ross THOMAS

Sheila WALSH
Romance

Barbara CARTLAND

Marion CHESNEY

Patricia ROBINS

Elizabeth SEIFERT

Joseph WAMBAUGH
Crime

Ed McBAIN

T. Jefferson PARKER

Marina WARNER
General

A.S. BYATT

Candia McWILLIAM

Keith WATERHOUSE
Humour

Kingsley AMIS

H.E. BATES

Malcolm BRADBURY

Michael DOBBS

David LODGE

Christopher MATTHEW

John MORTIMER

David NOBBS

Tom SHARPE

Leslie THOMAS

Peter TINNISWOOD

Sue TOWNSEND

P.G. WODEHOUSE

Paul WATKINS
General

Ernest HEMINGWAY

Erich Maria REMARQUE

Derek ROBINSON

William WHARTON

Colin WATSON
Crime

Simon BRETT

Edmund CRISPIN

Tim HEALD

James PATTINSON

Joyce PORTER

Ian WATSON
Science Fiction

Iain M. BANKS

J.G. BALLARD

Philip K. DICK

Auberon WAUGH
Humour

Henry CECIL

John MORTIMER

Nigel WILLIAMS

Evelyn WAUGH
General

Kingsley AMIS

E.F. BENSON

Malcolm BRADBURY

F. Scott FITZGERALD

Graham GREENE

Aldous HUXLEY

Anthony POWELL

C.P. SNOW

Muriel SPARK

P.G. WODEHOUSE

Anne WEALE
Romance

Lindsay ARMSTRONG

Penny JORDAN

Annabel MURRAY

Jan WEBSTER
Family Stories

Christine Marion FRASER

Maisie MOSCO

Frances PAIGE

Jessica STIRLING

Margaret WEIS
Fantasy

Terry BROOKS

David EDDINGS

Raymond E. FEIST

Fay WELDON
General

Margaret ATWOOD

Beryl BAINBRIDGE

Angela CARTER

Margaret DRABBLE

Margaret FORSTER

Penelope LIVELY

Alison LURIE

Deborah MOGGACH

Edna O'BRIEN

Wendy PERRIAM

Muriel SPARK

Emma TENNANT

Mary WESLEY

Jeanette WINTERSON

Patricia WENDORF
Historical

Cynthia HARROD-EAGLES

Malcolm MACDONALD

Pamela OLDFIELD

Claire RAYNER

E.V. THOMPSON

Patricia WENTWORTH
Crime

Catherine AIRD

Margery ALLINGHAM

Agatha CHRISTIE

Elizabeth GEORGE

Patricia WENTWORTH (cont.)

Martha GRIMES
Georgette HEYER
Emma LATHEN
Elizabeth LEMARCHAND
Gillian LINSCOTT
Ngaio MARSH
Jennie MELVILLE
Gladys MITCHELL
Gwen MOFFAT
Elizabeth PETERS
Dorothy L. SAYERS
June THOMSON
Michael UNDERWOOD

Mary WESLEY
General

Patricia ANGADI
Nina BAWDEN
Elizabeth BOWEN
Anita BROOKNER
Daphne DU MAURIER
Jane GARDAM
Mary HOCKING
Molly KEANE
Hilary MANTEL
Rosamunde PILCHER
Barbara PYM
Jean RHYS
Rose TREMAIN
Joanna TROLLOPE
Anne TYLER
Fay WELDON

Morris WEST
General

Saul BELLOW
Jon CLEARY
Frederick FORSYTH
Graham GREENE
Arthur HAILEY
David MALOUF
John MASTERS
W. Somerset MAUGHAM
Nevil SHUTE
Leon URIS
Frank YERBY

Rebecca WEST
General

Rosamond LEHMANN
Olivia MANNING

Donald WESTLAKE
Adventure

Richard CONDON
Leslie THOMAS
P.G. WODEHOUSE

Edith WHARTON
General

Henry JAMES

Nadine GORDIMER

V.S. NAIPAUL

William WHARTON
General

Joseph HELLER

Mary McCARTHY

Erich Maria REMARQUE

Paul WATKINS

Dennis WHEATLEY
Supernatural

Graham MASTERTON

John SAUL

Antonia WHITE
General

Edna O'BRIEN

Joanna TROLLOPE

Edmund WHITE
General

Michael CARSON

Alan HOLLINGHURST

Patrick WHITE
General

Peter CAREY

William GOLDING

Phyllis A. WHITNEY
Romance

Virginia COFFMAN

Ursula CURTISS

Dorothy EDEN

Winston GRAHAM

Isabelle HOLLAND

M.M. KAYE

Caroline LLEWELLYN

Barbara MICHAELS

Elizabeth PETERS

Anne STEVENSON

Mary STEWART

Daoma WINSTON

Philippa WIAT
Historical

Evelyn ANTHONY

Catherine GAVIN

Pamela HILL

Jean PLAIDY

John Edgar WIDEMAN
General

James BALDWIN

Chester B. HIMES

Charles WILLEFORD
Crime

Carl HIAASEN

Eugene IZZI

Tom KAKONIS

Elmore LEONARD

John D. MACDONALD

Walter MOSLEY

Jim THOMPSON

Andrew VACHSS

David WILLIAMS
Crime

Jonathan GASH

Alan HUNTER

Janet LAURENCE

Anne MORICE

Dee WILLIAMS
Family Stories

Harry BOWLING

Frances PAIGE

Rosie THOMAS

Barbara VICTOR

Gordon WILLIAMS
Humour

George Macdonald FRASER

Nigel WILLIAMS
Humour

Henry CECIL

Auberon WAUGH

Tad WILLIAMS
Fantasy

Marion Zimmer BRADLEY

David EDDINGS

Garry D. KILWORTH

Anne McCAFFREY

Henry WILLIAMSON
General

Richard ADAMS

William HORWOOD

A.R. LLOYD

Brian PARVIN

Anthony POWELL

Ernest RAYMOND

Erich Maria REMARQUE

Howard SPRING

David STEPHEN

Ted WILLIS
Family Stories

Harry BOWLING

Marie JOSEPH

Lena KENNEDY

Beryl KINGSTON

A.N. WILSON
General

Kingsley AMIS

Julian BARNES

Malcolm BRADBURY

Roy HATTERSLEY

Barbara PYM

Bernice RUBENS

Muriel SPARK

Angus WILSON
General

Malcolm BRADBURY

Anthony BURGESS

Graham GREENE

Iris MURDOCH

J.B. PRIESTLEY

Piers Paul READ

C.P. SNOW

Peter TAYLOR

David WILTSE
Crime

Mary Higgins CLARK

Thomas HARRIS

John WINGATE
Sea

Brian CALLISON

Sam LLEWELLYN

Philip McCUTCHAN

Dudley POPE

Douglas REEMAN

Antony TREW

R.D. WINGFIELD
Crime

Colin DEXTER

John HARVEY

Reginald HILL

Jonathan ROSS

David WINGROVE
Science Fiction

Frank HERBERT

Jack VANCE

Daoma WINSTON
Romance

Virginia ANDREWS

Carol CLEWLOW

Virginia COFFMAN

Janet DAILEY

Barbara MICHAELS

Daoma WINSTON (cont.)

Phyllis A. WHITNEY

Jeanette WINTERSON

Jeanette WINTERSON
General

Angela CARTER

Carol CLEWLOW

Colin THUBRON

Fay WELDON

Daoma WINSTON

John WINTON
Sea

Brian CALLISON

C.S. FORESTER

Max HENNESSY

Philip McCUTCHAN

Douglas REEMAN

Douglas SCOTT

P.G. WODEHOUSE
Humour

E.F. BENSON

Augustus CARP

Henry CECIL

Richard GORDON

Tom HOLT

Jerome K. JEROME

A.G. MACDONELL

David NOBBS

Peter TINNISWOOD

Keith WATERHOUSE

Evelyn WAUGH

Donald WESTLAKE

Gene WOLFE
Fantasy

Poul ANDERSON

Ray BRADBURY

Robert HOLDSTOCK

Ursula LE GUIN

Fritz LEIBER

Michael MOORCOCK

Tom WOLFE
General

Jay McINERNEY

Norman MAILER

Gore VIDAL

Ted WOOD
Crime

W.J. BURLEY

Michael UNDERWOOD

Sarah WOODHOUSE
Historical

Catherine GAVIN

Pamela OLDFIELD

E.V. THOMPSON

Daphne WRIGHT

Richard WOODMAN
Sea

Ronald BASSETT

Brian CALLISON

Bernard CORNWELL

C.S. FORESTER

Porter HILL

Alexander KENT

Philip McCUTCHAN

Dudley POPE

Showell STYLES

Sara WOODS
Crime

John Dickson CARR

Sarah CAUDWELL

Frances FYFIELD

Michael GILBERT

Anne MORICE

Emma PAGE

Dell SHANNON

Michael UNDERWOOD

Virginia WOOLF
General

Margaret ATWOOD

Iris MURDOCH

D.M. THOMAS

Herman WOUK
General

Howard FAST

Irwin SHAW

Daphne WRIGHT
General

M.M. KAYE

Sarah WOODHOUSE

Eric WRIGHT
Crime

Colin DEXTER

James MELVILLE

John WAINWRIGHT

Richard WRIGHT
General

James BALDWIN

Ralph ELLISON

William STYRON

Janny WURTS
Science Fiction

Anne McCAFFREY

Andre NORTON

John WYNDHAM
Science Fiction

Brian W. ALDISS

J.G. BALLARD

Iain M. BANKS

James BLISH

Ray BRADBURY

Harry HARRISON

Robert A. HEINLEIN

Frank HERBERT

Frederik POHL

Christopher PRIEST

Clifford D. SIMAK

Roger ZELAZNY

Frank YERBY
General

Margaret MITCHELL

Alexandra RIPLEY

Frank G. SLAUGHTER

Morris WEST

Margaret YORKE
Crime

Catherine AIRD

Sarah CAUDWELL

Ursula CURTISS

Elizabeth FERRARS

Antonia FRASER

Celia FREMLIN

Elizabeth GEORGE

Gerald HAMMOND

Patricia HIGHSMITH

Mary McMULLEN

Jessica MANN

Anne MORICE

Ruth RENDELL

Martin RUSSELL

Roger ZELAZNY
Science Fiction

Poul ANDERSON

Isaac ASIMOV

Ray BRADBURY

Jack L. CHALKER

Samuel R. DELANY

Gordon R. DICKSON

John WYNDHAM

AUTHORS LISTED BY GENRE

It is difficult to accurately identify individual authors with one particular section of genre fiction for often there is no 'cut off' point between, for instance, **War** and **Adventure;** between **Fantasy**, **Science Fiction** and the **Supernatural;** or between **Romance**, **Historical** and **Family Stories**. So, although in the main sequence this Guide indicates under the name of each author the genre in which they *usually* write and these names are repeated again in the lists that follow, it is suggested that readers also refer to linking genres and in particular to the list of **General** novelists to discover new names and new horizons. For this edition of the Guide only a broad statement of each genre has been used but in future editions it is hoped to sub-divide some of the categories, particularly **Crime**, **Science Fiction** and **Fantasy**, tc identify more specifically.

Do remember that some authors use a different name when they write in another genre and others will produce an occasional book quite different in character to their usual style. Always look at the book jacket and the introduction before you borrow or purchase.

Adventure

Stories that put the main character at risk of physical danger, often full of thrilling and daring feats, with most recent examples written at a fast pace. The cold war and its aftermath feature in many books of this type.

Ted ALLBEURY
Eric AMBLER
Evelyn ANTHONY
Jeffrey ARCHER
Campbell ARMSTRONG
Desmond BAGLEY
Larry BOND
Martin BOOTH
David BRIERLEY
John BUCHAN
Victor CANNING
Robert CARTER
Tom CLANCY
James CLAVELL
Jon CLEARY
Francis CLIFFORD
Richard CONDON
Robin COOK
Stephen COONTS
Bernard CORNWELL
Richard COX
Clive CUSSLER
Len DEIGHTON
Nelson DE MILLE
Peter DRISCOLL
Daniel EASTERMAN
Clive EGLETON
Gavin ESLER
Alan EVANS
Ian FLEMING
James FOLLETT
Ken FOLLETT
Colin FORBES
Frederick FORSYTH
Clare FRANCIS
Brian FREEMANTLE
Alexander FULLERTON
John GARDNER
Robert GODDARD
Nicholas GUILD
William HAGGARD
Arthur HAILEY
Adam HALL
Palma HARCOURT
John HARRIS
Michael HARTLAND
Jack HIGGINS
Geoffrey HOUSEHOLD
Christopher HYDE
Hammond INNES
Geoffrey JENKINS
Gary JENNINGS
Bob JUDD
John KATZENBACH
Philip KERR
Duncan KYLE

Derek LAMBERT
James LEASOR
John LE CARRÉ
Robert LITTELL
Robert LUDLAM
Gavin LYALL
Helen MACINNES
Alistair MACLEAN
J.K. MAYO
David MORRELL
Christopher NICOLE
Marc OLDEN
Harry PATTERSON
Thomas PERRY
Joe POYER
Anthony PRICE
Julian RATHBONE
Kenneth ROYCE
Ian ST JAMES
Lawrence SANDERS
Alan SAVAGE
Julian Jay SAVARIN
Tim SEBASTIAN
Owen SELA
Gerald SEYMOUR
Sidney SHELDON
Christopher SHERLOCK
Nevil SHUTE
Don SILVERMAN
Wilbur SMITH
Richard STARK
Douglas TERMAN
Craig THOMAS
John TRENHAILE
Elleston TREVOR
Eric VAN LUSTBADER
Leslie WALLER
Donald WESTLAKE

Crime - *including* ***Mysteries*** *and* ***Thrillers***

This type of novel is usually characterised by the placing of a number of clues which gradually lead the reader to the final solution often within an atmosphere of rising tension or danger. Some writers in this genre concentrate on the work of fictional police officers set in an actual police force situation. American police forces are usually shown working as a unit solving a number of crimes often set against a tough social background reflected in the characterisation and dialogue.

Catherine AIRD
Margery ALLINGHAM
Marian BABSON
Robert BARNARD
Linda BARNES
William BAYER
Josephine BELL
Nicholas BLAKE
Simon BRETT
Pat BURDEN
James Lee BURKE
W.J. BURLEY
Gwendoline BUTLER
James M. CAIN
Robert CAMPBELL
John Dickson CARR
Sarah CAUDWELL
John Newton CHANCE
Raymond CHANDLER
Leslie CHARTERIS
James Hadley CHASE
Agatha CHRISTIE
Douglas CLARK
Mary Higgins CLARK
Michael CLYNES
Liza CODY
Anthea COHEN
K.C. CONSTANTINE
Barry CORK
Patricia D. CORNWELL
William J. COUGHLIN
Robert CRAIS
John CREASEY
Edmund CRISPIN
Freeman Wills CROFTS
Amanda CROSS
Mark DANIEL
Lindsey DAVIS
Colin DEXTER
Michael DIBDIN
Peter DICKINSON
P.C. DOHERTY
Arthur DOUGLAS
Lesley EGAN
James ELLROY
Loren D. ESTLEMAN
Elizabeth EYRE
Elizabeth FERRARS
Robert FERRIGNO
Joy FIELDING

Dick FRANCIS
John FRANCOME
Antonia FRASER
Nicolas FREELING
Celia FREMLIN
Philip FRIEDMAN
Frances FYFIELD
Erle Stanley GARDNER
Jonathan GASH
Michael GELLER
Elizabeth GEORGE
Michael GILBERT
B.M. GILL
Robert GOLDSBOROUGH
Sue GRAFTON
James GRAHAM
Ann GRANGER
Lesley GRANT-ADAMSON
D.M. GREENWOOD
Martha GRIMES
John GRISHAM
James HALL
Dashiell HAMMETT
Gerald HAMMOND
Thomas HARRIS
Ray HARRISON
Roy HART
John HARVEY
S.T. HAYMON
Tim HEALD
Mark HEBDEN
Frances HEGARTY
Georgette HEYER
Patricia HIGHSMITH
Reginald HILL
Tony HILLERMAN
John Buxton HILTON
Alan HUNTER
Michael INNES
Eugene IZZI
Bill JAMES
P.D. JAMES
Roderic JEFFRIES
Katherine JOHN
Tom KAKONIS
Dan KAVANAGH
H.R.F. KEATING
Jonathan KELLERMAN
Susan KELLY
Judith KELMAN
William KIENZLE
Bill KNOX
Joseph KOENIG
Emma LATHEN
Janet LAURENCE
Elizabeth LEMARCHAND
Elmore LEONARD
David L. LINDSEY
Gillian LINSCOTT
Peter LOVESEY
Ed McBAIN
James McCLURE

Crime** - including **Mysteries** and **Thrillers (cont.)

John D. MACDONALD
Ross McDONALD
Mary McMULLEN
Jessica MANN
Ngaio MARSH
Steve MARTINI
James MELVILLE
Jennie MELVILLE
Gladys MITCHELL
Gwen MOFFAT
Susan MOODY
Anne MORICE
Walter MOSLEY
Patricia MOYES
Amy MYERS
Paul MYERS
Magdalen NABB
Janet NEEL
Roger ORMEROD
Emma PAGE
Sara PARETSKY
Robert B. PARKER
T. Jefferson PARKER
James PATTINSON
Michael PEARCE
Iain PEARS
Ridley PEARSON
John PENN
Ellis PETERS
Richard PITMAN
Joyce PORTER
Sheila RADLEY
Ruth RENDELL
Mike RIPLEY
C.F. ROE
Annette ROOME
Jonathan ROSS
Martin RUSSELL
Richard RUSSELL
Douglas RUTHERFORD
John SANDFORD
Dorothy L. SAYERS
Dell SHANNON
Simon SHAW
John SHERWOOD
Anita SHREVE
Georges SIMENON
Dorothy SIMPSON
Joan SMITH
Mickey SPILLANE
STAYNES & STOREY
Neville STEED
Rex STOUT
Whitley STRIEBER
Julian SYMONS
Josephine TEY
Ross THOMAS
Jim THOMPSON
June THOMSON
Mark TIMLIN

Michael TOLKIN
M.J. TROW
Peter TURNBULL
Scott TUROW
Michael UNDERWOOD
Andrew VACHSS
Barbara VINE
John WAINWRIGHT
Joseph WAMBAUGH
Colin WATSON
Patricia WENTWORTH
Charles WILLEFORD
David WILLIAMS
David WILTSE
R.D. WINGFIELD
Ted WOOD
Sara WOODS
Eric WRIGHT
Margaret YORKE

Family Stories

A popular genre frequently set against an historical background telling the story of two or more generations of a family with the plot often revolving around the purchase of property or the development of a family business. Included in this genre are **Family Sagas** in which the story is recorded in a number of volumes. There are close links to the **Historical** category with many authors writing in both genres.

Elizabeth ADLER
Charlotte Vale ALLEN
Lyn ANDREWS
Thomas ARMSTRONG
Hilary BAILEY
Tessa BARCLAY
Maeve BINCHY
Emma BLAIR
Philip BOAST
Harry BOWLING
Clare BOYLAN
Barbara Taylor BRADFORD
Brenda CLARKE
Virginia COFFMAN
Kathleen CONLON
Catherine COOKSON
Janet DAILEY
Elizabeth DAISH
Doris DAVIDSON
John Gordon DAVIS
Margaret Thomson DAVIS
Frank DELANEY
Mazo DE LA ROCHE
R.F. DELDERFIELD
Monica DICKENS
Jane DUNCAN
Rosemary ENRIGHT
Margaret ERSKINE
Zoe FAIRBAIRNS
Kate FLYNN
Helen FORRESTER
Christine Marion FRASER
Sara FRASER
Cynthia FREEMAN
Charles GIDLEY
Gail GODWIN
Suzanne GOODWIN
Iris GOWER
Margaret GRAHAM
Sarah HARRISON
Evelyn HOOD
Audrey HOWARD
Susan HOWATCH
Brenda JAGGER
Penny JORDAN
Marie JOSEPH
Sheelagh KELLY
Adam KENNEDY
Lena KENNEDY
Beryl KINGSTON
Claire LORRIMER
Malcolm MACDONALD

Hilda McKENZIE
Elisabeth McNEILL
Catherine MARCHANT
Anne MELVILLE
Mary MELWOOD
Mary MINTON
Connie MONK
Catrin MORGAN
Doris MORTMAN
Maisie MOSCO
Elizabeth MURPHY
Pamela OLDFIELD
Lewis ORDE
Frances PAIGE
Una-Mary PARKER
Mary E. PEARCE
Rosamunde PILCHER
Erin PIZZEY
Belva PLAIN
Deirdre PURCELL
Marjorie QUARTON
Claire RAYNER
Miss READ
Elvi RHODES
Ann Victoria ROBERTS
Denise ROBERTSON
Susan SALLIS
Judith SAXTON
Sarah SHEARS
Anne Rivers SIDDONS
Diana STAINFORTH
Mary Jane STAPLES
Danielle STEEL
Kay STEPHENS
D.E. STEVENSON
Caroline STICKLAND
Jessica STIRLING
Essie SUMMERS
Margaret SUNLEY
Jacqueline SUSANN
Reay TANNAHILL
Janet TANNER
Christine THOMAS
Rosie THOMAS
Grace THOMPSON
Nicola THORNE
Eileen TOWNSEND
Judy TURNER
Helen VAN SLYKE
Barbara VICTOR
Elizabeth VILLARS
Jan WEBSTER
Dee WILLIAMS
Ted WILLIS

Fantasy

Fantasy novels are based on the old folk tales and the gothic stories of the eighteenth and nineteenth centuries. Unlike Science Fiction they do not rely on technology but transport the reader to a magical world often linked to the Dark Ages.

Robert ADAMS
Robert ASPRIN
Jean M. AUEL
Clive BARKER
James P. BLAYCOCK
Robert BLOCH
Ray BRADBURY
Marion Zimmer BRADLEY
Terry BROOKS
Hugh COOK
Jamie DELANO
August DERLETH
Stephen DONALDSON
David EDDINGS
Raymond E. FEIST
Christopher FOWLER
Neil GAIMAN
David A. GEMMELL
Dave GIBBONS
Colin GREENLAND
Barbara HAMBLY
M. John HARRISON
Robert HOLDSTOCK
Robert JORDAN
Guy Gavriel KAY
Katherine KERR
Garry D. KILWORTH
Stephen KING
Stephen LAWS
Fritz LEIBER
C.S. LEWIS
H.P. LOVECRAFT
Nicholas LUARD
Brian LUMLEY
Anne McCAFFREY
Dan McGIRT
Richard MATHESON
Frank MILLER
Michael MOORCOCK
Alan MOORE
C.L. MOORE
Andre NORTON
Mervyn PEAKE
Terry PRATCHETT
Melanie RAWN
Tom REAMY
Keith ROBERTS
Dan SIMMONS
Clark Ashton SMITH
Mary STANTON
Christopher STASHEFF
Elizabeth M. THOMAS
J.R.R. TOLKIEN
John WAGNER
Margaret WEIS
Tad WILLIAMS
Gene WOLFE

General

Covers a great many authors for whom it is difficult or impossible to establish a genre. Within this **General** category will be found novels exploring personal relationships and the values and meaning of contemporary life. The setting may be in Britain or overseas. This category also includes authors whose plot and / or style change markedly from book to book. It also includes some authors whose writing has the characteristics of several genres.

Chinua ACHEBE
Peter ACKROYD
Richard ADAMS
Joan AIKEN
Isabel ALLENDE
Lisa ALTHER
Kingsley AMIS
Martin AMIS
Virginia ANDREWS
Patricia ANGADI
Margaret ATWOOD
Hilary BAILEY
Paul BAILEY
Beryl BAINBRIDGE
James BALDWIN
Lynne Reid BANKS
Russell BANKS
John BANVILLE
Noel BARBER
A.L. BARKER
Pat BARKER
Julian BARNES
Stan BARSTOW
H.E. BATES
Nina BAWDEN
Simon BELL
Saul BELLOW
Phyllis BENTLEY
Rachel BILLINGTON
Dirk BOGARDE
Elizabeth BOWEN
William BOYD
Malcolm BRADBURY
Melvyn BRAGG
John BRAINE
Andre BRINK
Anita BROOKNER
Brigid BROPHY
George Mackay BROWN
Anthony BURGESS
Anita BURGH
Betty BURTON
A.S. BYATT
Erskine CALDWELL
Taylor CALDWELL
Albert CAMUS
Ethan CANIN
Truman CAPOTE
Peter CAREY
Michael CARSON

General (cont.)

Angela CARTER
Brian CARTER
Joyce CARY
Bruce CHATWIN
Amit CHAUDHURI
John CHEEVER
Aeron CLEMENT
Carol CLEWLOW
Andrew COBURN
Ian COCHRANE
J.M. COETZEE
Jon COHEN
Isabel COLEGATE
Vernon COLEMAN
Norman COLLINS
Laurie COLWIN
Ivy COMPTON-BURNETT
Barbara COMYNS
Joseph CONRAD
David COOK
Lettice COOPER
William COOPER
Alexander CORDELL
Josephine COX
Michael CRICHTON
Julian CRITCHLEY
A.J. CRONIN
Susan CROSLAND
Robertson DAVIES
Bertie DENHAM
Henry DENKER
Anita DESAI
Jenny DISKI
Michael DOBBS
E.L. DOCTOROW
Anabel DONALD
J.P. DONLEAVY
Ellen DOUGLAS
Margaret DRABBLE
Daphne DU MAURIER
Lawrence DURRELL
Geoff DYER
Dorothy EDEN
Robert ELEGANT
Janice ELLIOTT
Alice Thomas ELLIS
Ralph ELLISON
Ben ELTON
Buchi EMECHETA
Sally EMERSON
Shusako ENDO
Louise ERDRICH
J.G. FARRELL
Howard FAST
William FAULKNER
Sebastian FAULKS
Anne FINE
F. Scott FITZGERALD
Penelope FITZGERALD
Ford Maddox FORD

Richard FORD
E.M. FORSTER
Margaret FORSTER
John FOWLES
Ronald FRAME
Marilyn FRENCH
Rosemary FRIEDMAN
Patrick GALE
Paul GALLICO
Janice GALLOWAY
John GALSWORTHY
Jane GARDAM
David GATES
Carlo GEBLER
Ellen GILCHRIST
Rumer GODDEN
William GOLDING
Nadine GORDIMER
Elizabeth GOUDGE
Winston GRAHAM
Günter GRASS
Robert GRAVES
Alasdair GRAY
Graham GREENE
Stephen GREGORY
John GRISHAM
David GROSSMAN
Rosa GUY
Rodney HALL
James HAMILTON-PATERSON
Georgina HAMMICK
Clare HARKNESS
Elizabeth HARRIS
Martyn HARRIS
L.P. HARTLEY
Roy HATTERSLEY
Joseph HELLER
Ernest HEMINGWAY
Herman HESSE
Carl HIAASEN
Susan HILL
Chester B. HIMES
Barry HINES
Mary HOCKING
Alice HOFFMAN
Ursula HOLDEN
Alan HOLLINGHURST
Winifred HOLTBY
Christopher HOPE
William HORWOOD
Elizabeth Jane HOWARD
Christopher HUDSON
Marsha HUNT
Aldous HUXLEY
Elspeth HUXLEY
John IRVING
Kazuo ISHIGURO
Howard JACOBSON
Rona JAFFE
Henry JAMES
Robin JENKINS

General (cont.)

Ruth Prawer JHABVALA
Pamela Hansford JOHNSON
Jennifer JOHNSTON
Elizabeth JOLLEY
Mervyn JONES
James JOYCE
Stuart M. KAMINSKY
M.M. KAYE
Molly KEANE
James KELMAN
Thomas KENEALLY
William KENNEDY
Jack KEROUAC
Ken KESEY
Arthur KOESTLER
Milan KUNDERA
Hanif KUREISHI
D.H. LAWRENCE
Harper LEE
Rosamond LEHMANN
Doris LESSING
Primo LEVI
Sinclair LEWIS
Penelope LIVELY
Caroline LLEWELLYN
Richard LLEWELLYN
A.R. LLOYD
David LODGE
Norah LOFTS
Russell LUCAS
Alison LURIE
Patrick McCABE
Mary McCARTHY
Carson McCULLERS
Colleen McCULLOUGH
Ian McEWAN
John McGAHERN
Jay McINERNEY
Shena MACKAY
Bernard MACLAVERTY
Terry McMILLAN
Larry McMURTRY
Candia McWILLIAM
Norman MAILER
Bernard MALAMUD
Michael MALONE
David MALOUF
Olivia MANNING
Hilary MANTEL
Gabriel Garcia MARQUEZ
Adam MARS-JONES
Bobbie Ann MASON
Allan MASSIE
John MASTERS
W. Somerset MAUGHAM
Armistead MAUPIN
Gita MEHTA
Barbara MICHAELS
James A. MICHENER
Paul MICOU

Stanley MIDDLETON
Sue MILLER
Yukio MISHIMA
Timothy MO
Deborah MOGGACH
Bel MOONEY
Brian MOORE
Lorrie MOORE
Mary MORRIS
Toni MORRISON
Penelope MORTIMER
Alice MUNRO
Haruki MURAKAMI
Iris MURDOCH
Vladimir NABOKOV
V.S. NAIPAUL
R.K. NARAYAN
Gloria NAYLOR
Robert NYE
Ann OAKLEY
Joyce Carol OATES
Edna O'BRIEN
Flann O'BRIEN
Flannery O'CONNOR
Frank O'CONNOR
Sean O'FAOLAIN
John O'HARA
Ben OKRI
Michael ONDAATJE
George ORWELL
Amos OZ
Joy PACKER
Elizabeth PALMER
Brian PARVIN
Alan PATON
Wendy PERRIAM
Elizabeth PETERS
K.M. PEYTON
Caryl PHILLIPS
Marge PIERCY
Chaim POTOK
Anthony POWELL
Amanda PRANTERA
J.B. PRIESTLEY
V.S. PRITCHETT
Mario PUZO
Barbara PYM
Frederic RAPHAEL
Ernest RAYMOND
Piers Paul READ
Erich Maria REMARQUE
Mary RENAULT
Jean RHYS
Jane ROGERS
Judith ROSSNER
Philip ROTH
Bernice RUBENS
Salman RUSHDIE
J.D. SALINGER
Paul SAYER
Paul SCOTT
Vikram SETH

General (cont.)

- Margery SHARP
- Irwin SHAW
- Antony SHER
- Carol SHIELDS
- Alan SILLITOE
- Isaac Bashevis SINGER
- Frank G. SLAUGHTER
- Jane SMILEY
- Iain Crichton SMITH
- C.P. SNOW
- Muriel SPARK
- Howard SPRING
- Marguerite STEEN
- John STEINBECK
- David STEPHEN
- J.I.M. STEWART
- Mary STEWART
- David STOREY
- Jean STUBBS
- William STYRON
- Graham SWIFT
- Elizabeth TAYLOR
- Peter TAYLOR
- Emma TENNANT
- Paul THEROUX
- Angela THIRKELL
- D.M. THOMAS
- Leslie THOMAS
- Colin THUBRON
- Gillian TINDALL
- Rose TREMAIN
- William TREVOR
- Joanna TROLLOPE
- Anne TYLER
- Barry UNSWORTH
- John UPDIKE
- Leon URIS
- Denys VAL BAKER
- Alice WALKER
- Marina WARNER
- Paul WATKINS
- Evelyn WAUGH
- Fay WELDON
- Mary WESLEY
- Morris WEST
- Rebecca WEST
- Edith WHARTON
- William WHARTON
- Antonia WHITE
- Edmund WHITE
- Patrick WHITE
- John Edgar WIDEMAN
- Henry WILLIAMSON
- A.N. WILSON
- Angus WILSON
- Jeanette WINTERSON
- Tom WOLFE
- Virginia WOOLF
- Herman WOUK
- Daphne WRIGHT
- Richard WRIGHT
- Frank YERBY

Historical

Another very popular category where fictional characters are set against an actual historical perspective with close and realistic links between fiction and fact. Many of the books in this genre have a romantic theme and some libraries have a separate sequence of **Historical Romances**.

Valerie ANAND
Evelyn ANTHONY
Pamela BELLE
Gillian BRADSHAW
Madeleine BRENT
D.K. BROSTER
Elizabeth BYRD
Philippa CARR
Elizabeth CHADWICK
Teresa CRANE
Emma DRUMMOND
Dorothy DUNNETT
Barbara ERSKINE
Catherine GASKIN
Catherine GAVIN
Valerie GEORGESON
Judith GLOVER
Winston GRAHAM
Barbara HAMLYN
Cynthia HARROD-EAGLES
Georgette HEYER
Pamela HILL
Jane Aiken HODGE
Isabelle HOLLAND
Victoria HOLT
Sara HYLTON
Rosalind LAKER
Dinah LAMPITT
Morgan LLYWELYN
Genevieve LYONS
Margaret MITCHELL
Neil MUNRO
Diana NORMAN
Edith PARGETER
Diane PEARSON
Margaret PEMBERTON
Sharon PENMAN
Jean PLAIDY
J.M. RILEY
Alexandra RIPLEY
Carola SALISBURY
Anya SETON
Vivian STUART
Rosemary SUTCLIFF
E.V. THOMPSON
Nigel TRANTER
Gore VIDAL
Patricia WENDORF
Philippa WIAT
Sarah WOODHOUSE

Humour

A select group of authors whose novels are mainly written to amuse.

H.E. BATES
Guy BELLAMY
E.F. BENSON
Augustus CARP
Henry CECIL
Roy CLARKE
Colin DOUGLAS
Roddy DOYLE
George Macdonald FRASER
Michael FRAYN
Richard GORDON
George GROSSMITH
Tom HOLT
Jerome K. JEROME
Garrison KEILLOR
A.G. MACDONELL
Christopher MATTHEW
John MORTIMER
David NOBBS
Barry PAIN
Nicholas SALAMAN
Tom SHARPE
Peter TINNISWOOD
Sue TOWNSEND
Keith WATERHOUSE
Auberon WAUGH
Gordon WILLIAMS
Nigel WILLIAMS
P.G. WODEHOUSE

Romance

Novels usually written by women for women with a romantic theme. Some writers specialise in historical settings but for the purposes of this guide the major theme determines the genre. Many libraries will have a separate section of shelves for **Romance**.

Lucilla ANDREWS
Lindsay ARMSTRONG
Iris BROMIGE
Elizabeth CADELL
Barbara CARTLAND
Marion CHESNEY
Caroline COURTNEY
Ursula CURTISS
Clare DARCY
Emma DARCY
Joyce DINGWELL
Jane DONNELLY
Catherine GEORGE
Rosemary HAMMOND
Stephanie HOWARD
Charlotte LAMB
Judith McNAUGHT
Audrie MANLEY-TUCKER
Anne MATHER
Carole MORTIMER
Annabel MURRAY
Betty NEELS
Lilian PEAKE
Denise ROBINS
Patricia ROBINS
Elizabeth SEIFERT
Jessica STEELE
Anne STEVENSON
Elswyth THANE
Kay THORPE
Sheila WALSH
Anne WEALE
Phyllis A. WHITNEY
Daoma WINSTON

Science Fiction

Books in this genre are set in the future exploring scientific ideas and advanced technology.

Douglas ADAMS
Brian W. ALDISS
Poul ANDERSON
Piers ANTHONY
Isaac ASIMOV
J.G. BALLARD
Iain M. BANKS
Greg BEAR
James BLISH
David BRIN
John BRUNNER
Pat CADIGAN
Orson Scott CARD
Jack L. CHALKER
C.J. CHERRYH
Arthur C. CLARKE
Richard COWPER
Samuel R. DELANY
Philip K. DICK
Gordon R. DICKSON
Harlan ELLISON
Philip Jose FARMER
Alan Dean FOSTER
Mary GENTLE
William GIBSON
Joe HALDEMAN
Harry HARRISON
Robert A. HEINLEIN
Frank HERBERT
James P. HOGAN
Tom HOLT
K.W. JETER
Gwyneth JONES
Ursula LE GUIN
Stanislaw LEM
Vonda N. MACINTYRE
Julian MAY
Grant NAYLOR
Larry NIVEN
Frederik POHL
Christopher PRIEST
Robert RANKIN
Kim Stanley ROBINSON
Rudy RUCKER
Joanna RUSS
Eric Frank RUSSELL
Fred SABERHAGEN
Bob SHAW
Robert SHECKLEY
Robert SILVERBERG
Clifford D. SIMAK
Brian STABLEFORD
Bruce STERLING
Sheri S. TEPPER
Jack VANCE
Ian WATSON
David WINGROVE
Janny WURTS
John WYNDHAM
Roger ZELAZNY

Sea

A popular category where many authors have made a well-deserved reputation for writing about the sea either in an historical or contemporary setting. Many novelists in this genre will also be found under **Adventure** and also under **War Stories**.

Ronald BASSETT
Brian CALLISON
Eric J. COLLENETTE
C.S. FORESTER
Raymond HARDIE
Porter HILL
Alexander KENT
A.E. LANGSFORD
Sam LLEWELLYN
Philip McCUTCHAN
Nicholas MONSARRAT
Patrick O'BRIAN
Dudley POPE
Douglas REEMAN
Douglas SCOTT
Showell STYLES
Victor SUTHREN
Peter TONKIN
Antony TREW
John WINGATE
John WINTON
Richard WOODMAN

The 'Smart Set'

A fairly recent phenomenon, this genre features the modern world of big business and entertainment with generous proportions of sex, violence and avarice. Identified in libraries and bibliographies by a number of alternative headings including 'Contemporary Glamour'.

Sally BEAUMAN
Pat BOOTH
Celia BRAYFIELD
Freda BRIGHT
Jacqueline BRISKIN
Sandra BROWN
Julie BURCHILL
Jackie COLLINS
Joan COLLINS
Shirley CONRAN
Jilly COOPER
Julie ELLIS
Elizabeth GAGE
Judith GOULD
Sarah HARRISON
Burt HIRSCHFIELD
Judith KRANTZ
Lynda LA PLANTE
Molly PARKIN
Harold ROBBINS
June Flaum SINGER
Jacqueline SUSANN
Barbara TRAPIDO
Thomas TRYON
Penny VINCENZI

Supernatural and the Unknown

This section includes authors who frequently write suspense and horror where the story line involves pursuit and eventual escape often from the supernatural, demonic or the occult.

Jonathan AYCLIFFE
Ramsey CAMPBELL
Nancy COLLINS
John FARRIS
Stephen GALLAGHER
Steve HARRIS
James HERBERT
Shaun HUTSON
Peter JAMES
Stephen KING
Dean R. KOONTZ
Richard LAYMON
Robert McCAMMON
George R. MARTIN
Graham MASTERTON
Mark MORRIS
Kim NEWMAN
Anne RICE
Philip RICKMAN
John SAUL
Guy N. SMITH
Peter STRAUB
Dennis WHEATLEY

War Stories

Authors who have written widely but not exclusively about war generally within the 19th and 20th centuries. Many books about war will also be found under **Adventure** and **Sea Stories**. Some novelists listed in the **General** category have also written individual books about war.

Peter ABRAHAMS

Larry FORRESTER

W.E.B. GRIFFIN

John HARRIS

Max HENNESSY

Richard HOUGH

Robert JACKSON

Hans Helmut KIRST

Derek ROBINSON

Terence STRONG

L.K. TRUSCOTT

Western

Books set in the old American West with a range of plots from romance to adventure. Only a selection of the many authors who write in this genre are included in the Guide and, as with **Romance** many libraries will have a separate section for **Western Stories**.

Max BRAND
Matt CHISHOLM
Al CODY
Jess CODY
J.T. EDSON
Zane GREY
Wade HAMILTON
Louis L'AMOUR
Chuck MARTIN
Nelson NYE
Clint OGDEN
T.C. OLSEN
Lauran PAINE
Gary PAULSEN
Jack SCHAEFER
Bill WADE

LITERARY PRIZES AND AWARDS

There are well over 200 prizes and awards currently on offer to writers and publishers. The following list, covers the period from 1970 to date and contains most of those for which works of fiction are eligible. Further information on the awards themselves, but not the complete list of prize winners, may be found in the **Guide to Literary Prizes, Grants and Awards in Britain and Ireland** (Book Trust/Society of Authors, 1992); **The Writers and Artists Year Book,** (A & C Black, 1993) or in **The Writer's Handbook, edited by Barry Turner** (Macmillan, 1993).

AUTHORS' CLUB FIRST NOVEL AWARD

This is given to the most promising First Novel published by a writer in Great Britain. Introduced by Laurence Meynell in 1954.

1980	Barbara BENSON	The Underlings
1981	Katharine GORDON	The Emerald Peacock
1982	Martin PAGE	The Pilate Plot
1983	Dawn LOWE-WATSON	The Good Morrow
1984	Anne SMITH	The Magic Glass
1985	Frances VERNON	Privileged Children
1986	Katherine MOORE	Summer at the Haven
1987	Frederick HYDE-CHAMBERS	Lama, a Story of Tibet
1988	Magda SWEETLAND	Eightsome Reel
1989	Helen HARRIS	Playing Fields in Winter
1990	Peter BENSON	The Levels
1991	Alan BROWNJOHN	The Way You Tell Them
1992	Zina ROHAN	The Book of Wishes and Complaints

JAMES TAIT BLACK MEMORIAL PRIZES

The James Tait Black Memorial Prizes, founded in memory of a partner in the publishing house A & C Black Ltd, were instituted in 1918. Two prizes are awarded annually: one for the best biography or work of that type and the other for the best work of fiction published during the calendar year.

	Year	Author	Title
joint winners	1981	Salman RUSHDIE	Midnight's Children
	1981	Paul THEROUX	The Mosquito Coast
	1982	Bruce CHATWIN	On the Black Hill
	1983	Jonathan KEATES	Allegro Postillions
joint winners	1984	J.G. BALLARD	Empire of the Sun
	1984	Angela CARTER	Nights at the Circus
	1985	Robert EDRIC	Winter Garden
	1986	Jenny JOSEPH	Persephone
	1987	George Mackay BROWN	The Golden Bird: Two Orkney Stories
	1988	Piers Paul READ	A Season in the West
	1989	James KELMAN	A Disaffection
	1990	William BOYD	Brazzaville Beach
	1991	Iain SINCLAIR	Downriver
	1992	Rose TREMAIN	Sacred Country

BOARDMAN TASKER AWARD FOR MOUNTAIN LITERATURE

This award commemorates the lives of Peter Boardman and Joe Tasker and is given to the author of an original work, either fiction or non-fiction, which has made an outstanding contribution to mountain literature. Since its inception in 1983 two novels have won the award:-

1989	M. John HARRISON	Climbers
1991	Alison FELL	Mer de Glace

BOOKER PRIZE FOR FICTION

Established in 1968 by Booker McConnell Ltd., eligible novels must be written in English by a citizen of Britain, the Commonwealth, the Republic of Ireland or South Africa.

The announcement of the winner has been televised live since 1981.

	Year	Author	Title
	1969	P.H. NEWBY	Something to Answer For
	1970	Bernice RUBENS	The Elected Member
	1971	V.S. NAIPAUL	In a Free State
	1972	John BERGER	G
	1973	J.G. FARRELL	The Siege of Krishnapur
joint winners	1974	Nadine GORDIMER	The Conservationist
joint winners	1974	Stanley MIDDLETON	Holiday
	1975	Ruth Prawer JHABVALA	Heat and Dust
	1976	David STOREY	Seville
	1977	Paul SCOTT	Staying On
	1978	Iris MURDOCH	The Sea, The Sea
	1979	Penelope FITZGERALD	Offshore
	1980	William GOLDING	Rites of Passage
	1981	Salman RUSHDIE	Midnight's Children
	1982	Thomas KENEALLY	Schindler's Ark
	1983	J.M. COETZEE	Life & Times of Michael K
	1984	Anita BROOKNER	Hotel du Lac
	1985	Keri HULME	The Bone People
	1986	Kingsley AMIS	The Old Devils
	1987	Penelope LIVELY	Moon Tiger
	1988	Peter CAREY	Oscar and Lucinda
	1989	Kazuo ISHIGURO	The Remains of the Day
	1990	A.S. BYATT	Possession
	1991	Ben OKRI	The Famished Road
joint winners	1992	Michael ONDAATJE	The English Patient
joint winners	1992	Barry UNSWORTH	Sacred Hunger

BRITISH FANTASY AWARDS

Originally termed the August Derleth Fantasy Award, the British Fantasy Society announced its first award in 1972 for the best novel of the previous year.

1971	Michael MOORCOCK	The Knight of the Swords
1972	Michael MOORCOCK	The King of the Swords
1973	Poul ANDERSON	Hrolf Kraki's Saga
1974	Michael MOORCOCK	The Sword and the Stallion
1975	Michael MOORCOCK	The Hollow Lands
1976	Gordon DICKSON	The Dragon and the George
1977	Piers ANTHONY	A Spell for Chameleon
1978	Stephen DONALDSON	The Chronicles of Thomas Covenant
1979	Tanith LEE	Death's Master
1980	Ramsey CAMPBELL	To Wake the Dead
1981	Stephen KING	Cujo
1982	Gene WOLFE	Sword of the Lictor
1983	Peter STRAUB	Floating Dragon
1984	Ramsey CAMPBELL	Incarnate
1985	T.E.D. KLEIN	The Ceremonies
1986	Stephen KING	It
1987	Ramsey CAMPBELL	The Hungry Moon
1988	Ramsey CAMPBELL	The Influence
1989	Dan SIMMONS	Carrion Comfort
1990	Ramsey CAMPBELL	Midnight Sun
1991	Jonathan CARROLL	Outside the Dog Museum

BRITISH SCIENCE FICTION AWARD

Awarded annually, after a ballot of members, by the British Science Fiction Association. Given in four categories: Best Novel; Best Short Fiction; Best Media Presentation; and Best Artwork. Novel winners since 1982 are:-

1982	Gene WOLFE	The Shadow of the Torturer
1983	Brian ALDISS	Helliconia Spring
1984	John SLADEK	Tik-Tok
1985	Robert HOLDSTOCK	Mythago Wood
1986	Brian ALDISS	Helliconia Winter
1987	Bob SHAW	The Ragged Astronauts
1988	Keith ROBERTS	Grainne
1989	Robert HOLDSTOCK	Lavondyss
1990	Terry PRATCHETT	Pyramids
1991	Colin GREENLAND	Take Back Plenty
1992	Dan SIMMONS	The Fall of Hyperion

ARTHUR C. CLARKE AWARD

This award, established in 1986, is for a Science Fiction novel and there are no limits on country of origin.

Horror and Fantasy are excluded unless there is a strong SF element in the book.

1987	Margaret ATWOOD	The Handmaid's Tale
1988	George TURNER	The Sea and Summer
1989	Rachel POLLACK	Unquenchable Fire
1990	Geoff RYMAN	The Child Garden
1991	Colin GREENLAND	Take Back Plenty
1992	Pat CADIGAN	Synners
1993	Marge PIERCY	Body of Glass

DAVID COHEN BRITISH LITERATURE PRIZE

This latest award is supported and administered by the Arts Council of Great Britain. The prize money is put up by the David Cohen Family Charitable Trust. It is awarded every two years for a lifetime of achievement to a distinguished writer of British citizenship who works in the English, Gaelic, or Welsh languages.

1993 Sir Vidia NAIPAUL

COMMONWEALTH WRITERS PRIZE

Established in 1987 by the Commonwealth Foundation in association with the Book Trust and the Royal Overseas League, the award is administered annually within one of four regions of the Commonwealth. Entries submitted by publishers must be novels or short stories.

1987	Olive SENIOR	Summer Lightning
1988	Festus IYAYI	Heroes
1989	Janet FRAME	The Carpathians
1990	Mordecai RICHLER	Soloman Gursky
1991	David MALOUF	The Great World
1992	Rohinton MISTRY	Such a Long Journey

CATHERINE COOKSON FICTION PRIZE

A new award founded in 1992 by Transworld Publishers to celebrate the achievement of Catherine Cookson.

Awarded to a novel of at least 70,000 words in length that possesses features of strong characterisation, authentic background and story telling ability.

1993	Valerie WOOD	The Sea is my Companion

CRIME WRITERS' ASSOCIATION

The first meeting of the Association was convened by John Creasey in November 1953 and awards have been presented since 1955 for the best crime novel of the year. Originally called the Crossed Red Herrings Award it is now the Gold Dagger. The Silver Dagger goes to the runner up. The John Creasey Memorial Award (JCMA), instituted to commemorate his death in 1973, is for the best crime novel by an author who has not previously published a full length work of fiction. From 1985 to 1987, the Police Review sponsored an award for the crime novel which best portrayed police work and procedure. In 1988 for one year only, Punch magazine sponsored a prize for the funniest crime book of the year. It has now been superseded by The Last Laugh Award. In 1990, Hazel Wynn Jones instituted the CWA '92 Award to run for three years for a crime novel partly or wholly set in Europe. Also in 1990 the New Law Journal sponsored the biennial Rumpole Award for a crime novel with a British legal setting. All these awards are set out below under each year.

1970	Joan FLEMING	*Gold Dagger*	Young Man I Think You're Dying
	Anthony PRICE	*Silver Dagger*	The Labyrinth Makers
1971	James McCLURE	*Gold Dagger*	The Steam Pig
	P.D. JAMES	*Silver Dagger*	Shroud for a Nightingale
1972	Eric AMBLER	*Gold Dagger*	The Levanter
	Victor CANNING	*Silver Dagger*	The Rainbird Pattern
1973	Robert LITTELL	*Gold Dagger*	The Defection of A.J. Lewinter
	Gwendoline BUTLER	*Silver Dagger*	A Coffin for Pandora
	Kyril BONFIGLIOLI	*J.C.M.A.*	Don't Point That Thing at Me

CRIME WRITERS' ASSOCIATION (cont.)

1974	Anthony Price	*Gold Dagger*	Other Paths to Glory
	Francis CLIFFORD	*Silver Dagger*	The Grosvenor Square Goodbye
	Roger L. SIMON	*J.C.M.A.*	The Big Fix
1975	Nicholas MEYER	*Gold Dagger*	The Seven Per Cent Solution
	P.D. JAMES	*Silver Dagger*	The Black Tower
	Sara GEORGE	*J.C.M.A.*	Acid Drop
1976	Ruth RENDELL	*Gold Dagger*	A Demon in my View
	James McCLURE	*Silver Dagger*	Rogue Eagle
	Patrick ALEXANDER	*J.C.M.A.*	Death of a Thin Skinned Animal
1977	John LE CARRÉ	*Gold Dagger*	The Honourable Schoolboy
	William McILVANNEY	*Silver Dagger*	Laidlaw
	Jonathan GASH	*J.C.M.A.*	The Judas Pair
1978	Lionel DAVIDSON	*Gold Dagger*	The Chelsea Murders
	Peter LOVESEY	*Silver Dagger*	Waxwork
	Paula GOSLING	*J.C.M.A.*	A Running Duck
1979	Dick FRANCIS	*Gold Dagger*	Whip Hand
	Colin DEXTER	*Silver Dagger*	Service of all the Dead
	David SERAFIN	*J.C.M.A.*	Saturday of Glory
1980	H.R.F. KEATING	*Gold Dagger*	The Murder of the Maharajah
	Ellis PETERS	*Silver Dagger*	Monk's Hood
	Liza CODY	*J.C.M.A.*	Dupe

CRIME WRITERS' ASSOCIATION (cont.)

Year	Author	Award	Title
1981	Martin Cruz SMITH	*Gold Dagger*	Gorky Park
	Colin DEXTER	*Silver Dagger*	The Dead of Jericho
	James LEIGH	*J.C.M.A.*	The Ludi Victor
1982	Peter LOVESEY	*Gold Dagger*	The False Inspector Dew
	S.T. HAYMON	*Silver Dagger*	Ritual Murder
	Andrew TAYLOR	*J.C.M.A.*	Caroline Minuscule
1983	John HUTTON	*Gold Dagger*	Accidental Crimes
	William McILVANNEY	*Silver Dagger*	The Papers of Tony Veitch
Tied	Carol CLEMEAU	*J.C.M.A.*	The Ariadne Clue
Tied	Eric WRIGHT	*J.C.M.A.*	The Night the Gods Smiled
1984	B.M. GILL	*Gold Dagger*	The Twelfth Juror
	Ruth RENDELL	*Silver Dagger*	The Tree of Hands
	Elizabeth IRONSIDE	*J.C.M.A.*	A Very Private Enterprise
1985	Paula GOSLING	*Gold Dagger*	Monkey Puzzle
	Dorothy SIMPSON	*Silver Dagger*	Last Seen Alive
	Robert RICHARDSON	*J.C.M.A.*	The Latimer Mercy
	Andrew ARNCLIFFE	*Police Review Award*	After the holiday
1986	Ruth RENDELL	*Gold Dagger*	Live Flesh
	P.D. JAMES	*Silver Dagger*	A Taste for Death
	Neville STEED	*J.C.M.A.*	Tinplate
	Bill KNOX	*Police Review Award*	The Crossfire Killings

CRIME WRITERS' ASSOCIATION (cont.)

Year	Author	Award	Title
1987	Barbara VINE	*Gold Dagger*	A Fatal Inversion
	Scott TUROW	*Silver Dagger*	Presumed Innocent
	Denis KILCOMMONS	*J.C.M.A.*	Dark Apostle
	Roger BUSBY	*Police Review Award*	Snowman
1988	Michael DIBDIN	*Gold Dagger*	Ratking
	Sara PARETSKY	*Silver Dagger*	Toxic Shock
	Janet NEEL	*J.C.M.A.*	Death's Bright Angel
	Nancy LIVINGSTON	*Punch Prize*	Death in a Distant Land
1989	Colin DEXTER	*Gold Dagger*	The Wench is Dead
	Desmond LOWDEN	*Silver Dagger*	The Shadow Run
	Annette ROOME	*J.C.M.A.*	A Real Shot in the Arm
	Mike RIPLEY	*Last Laugh Award*	Angel Touch
1990	Reginald HILL	*Gold Dagger*	Bones and Silence
	Mike PHILLIPS	*Silver Dagger*	The Late Candidate
	Patricia Daniels CORNWELL	*J.C.M.A.*	Postmortem
	Simon SHAW	*Last Laugh Award*	Killer Cinderella
	Michael DIBDIN	*CWA '92 Award*	Vendetta
	Frances FYFIELD	*Rumpole Award*	Trial by Fire
1991	Barbara VINE	*Gold Dagger*	King Solomon's Carpet
	Frances FYFIELD	*Silver Dagger*	Deep Sleep
	Walter MOSLEY	*J.C.M.A.*	Devil in a Blue Dress
	Mike RIPLEY	*Last Laugh Award*	Angels in Arms
	Barbara WILSON	*CWA '92 Award*	Gaudi Afternoon

1992	Colin DEXTER	*Gold Dagger*	The Way Through the Woods
	Liza CODY	*Silver Dagger*	Bucket Nut
	Minette WALTERS	*J.C.M.A.*	The Ice House
	Carl HIAASEN	*Last Laugh Award*	Native Tongue
	Timothy WILLIAMS	*CWA '92 Award*	Black August
	Peter RAWLINSON	*Rumpole Award*	Hatred and Contempt

GEOFFREY FABER MEMORIAL PRIZE

As a memorial to the founder and first Chairman of the firm, Faber and Faber Limited established the prize in 1963. Awarded annually it is given in alternate years for a volume of verse and for a volume of prose fiction published originally in this country by writers who are under 40 years of age. The following is the list of fiction prize winners:-

1971	J.G. FARRELL	Troubles
1973	David STOREY	Pasmore
1975	Richard WRIGHT	The Middle of a Life
1977	Carolyn SLAUGHTER	The Story of the Weasel
1979	Timothy MO	The Monkey King
1981	J.M. COETZEE	Waiting for the Barbarians
1983	Graham SWIFT	Shuttlecock
1985	Julian BARNES	Flaubert's Parrot
1987	Guy VANDERHAEGHE	Man Descending
1989	David PROFUMO	Sea Music
1991	Carol BIRCH	The Fog Line
1993	Will SELF	The Quantity Theory of Insanity

FAWCETT SOCIETY BOOK PRIZE

An annual award, made until 1993 alternately to a work of fiction and non-fiction, which has made a substantial contribution to the understanding of women's concerns, attitudes and place in society. From 1993 the prize will always be awarded to a work of non-fiction.

1983	Pat BARKER	Union Street
1985	Zoe FAIRBAIRNS	Here Today
1987	Shena MACKAY	Redhill Rococo
1989	Stevie SMITH	Boy Blue
1991	Jennifer DAWSON	Judasland

HAWTHORNDEN PRIZE

Founded in 1919 by Miss Alice Warrender, it is the oldest of the famous British literary prizes. Awarded annually to an English writer for the best work of imaginative literature, it is especially designed to encourage young authors and the word 'imaginative' is given a broad interpretation.

The following dates are the years for which the award was given to a work of fiction:-

1970	Piers Paul READ	Monk Dawson
1975	David LODGE	Changing Places
1976	Robert NYE	Falstaff
1978	David COOK	Walter
1979	P.S. RUSHFORTH	Kindergarten
1982	Timothy MO	Sour Sweet
1983	Jonathan KEATES	Allegro Postillions
1992	Ferdinand MOUNT	Of Love and Asthma
1993	Andrew BARROW	The Tap Dancer

HEINEMANN FICTION AWARD

Founded in 1990 in partnership with East Midlands and Eastern Regional Arts Boards. The biennial award aims to promote new writing in the Eastern and East Midlands regions .

1990	Alison ANTHONY	Strange Malady
1992	Brendan MURPHY	Call me Sweetbriar

DAVID HIGHAM PRIZE FOR FICTION

An annual award for a first novel or book of short stories published in the UK in the year of the award, by an author who is a citizen of Britain, the Commonwealth, the Republic of Ireland or South Africa.

	Year	Author	Title
joint winners	1975	Jane GARDAM	Black Faces/White Faces
	1975	Matthew VAUGHAN	Chalky
	1976	Caroline BLACKWOOD	The Stepdaughter
	1977	Patricia FINNEY	A Shadow of Gulls
	1978	Leslie NORRIS	Sliding
	1979	John HARVEY	The Plate Shop
	1980	Ted HARRIOT	Keep on Running
	1981	Christopher HOPE	A Separate Development
	1982	Glyn HUGHES	Where I Used to Play on the Green
	1983	R.M. LAMMING	The Notebook of Gismondo Cavalletti
	1984	James BUCHAN	A Parish of Rich Women
	1985	Patricia FERGUSON	Family Myths and Legends
	1986	Jim CRACE	Continent
	1987	Adam ZAMEENZAD	The 13th House
	1988	Carol BIRCH	Life in the Palace
	1989	Timothy O'GRADY	Motherland
	1990	Russell Celyn JONES	Soldiers and Innocents
	1991	Elspeth BARKER	O Caledonia
	1992	John LOVEDAY	Halo

WINIFRED HOLTBY MEMORIAL PRIZE

In 1966 Vera Brittain gave to the Royal Society of Literature a sum of money to provide an annual prize in honour of Winifred Holtby. It is for the best regional novel of the year written in the English Language. Winners since 1981 are:-

1981	Elsa JOUBERT	Poppie
1982	Alan JUDD	A Breed of Heroes
1983	Kazuo ISHIGURO	A Pale View of Hills
1984	Graham SWIFT	Waterland
1985	Balraj KHANNA	Nation of Fools
1986	*No Award*	
1987	Maggie HEMINGWAY	The Bridge
1988	Susha GUPPY	The Blindfold Horse
1989	Hilary MANTEL	Fludd
1990	Nino RICCI	The Lives of the Saints
1991	Elspeth BARKER	O Caledonia

MAIL ON SUNDAY / JOHN LLEWELLYN RHYS PRIZE

Founded in 1942 by Jane Oliver, the widow of John Llewellyn Rhys a young writer killed in action in World War II. Open to writers aged under 35 the work may be any form of literature:- fiction, short stories, poetry, drama, biography or literary non-fiction written by a British or Commonwealth writer.

1970	*No Award to Fiction*	
1971	Shiva NAIPAUL	Fireflies
1972	Susan HILL	The Albatross
1973	Peter SMALLEY	A Warm Gun
1974	Hugh FLEETWOOD	The Girl who Passed for Normal
1975	Tim JEAL	Cushing's Crusade
1976	*No Award*	
1977	*No Award to Fiction*	
1978	A.N. WILSON	The Sweets of Pimlico
1979	*No Award to Fiction*	
1980	Desmond HOGAN	The Diamonds at the Bottom of the Sea
1981	*No Award to Fiction*	
1982	William BOYD	An Ice-Cream War
1983	Lisa ST AUBIN DE TERAN	The Slow Train to Milan
1984	*No Award to Fiction*	
1985	John MILNE	Out of the Blue
1986	Tim PARKS	Loving Roger
1987	Jeanette WINTERSON	The Passion
1988	Matthew YORKE	The March Fence
1989	*No Award to Fiction*	
1990	*No Award to Fiction*	
1991	*No Award to Fiction*	
1992	Matthew KNEALE	Sweet Thames

PULITZER PRIZE FOR FICTION

Joseph Pulitzer, reporter, editor, publisher and a founder of the Graduate School of Journalism at Columbia University established in 1903 a system of prizes to encourage 'public service, public morals, American literature and the advancement of education'. The Fiction Prize was first awarded in 1948.

1970	Jean STAFFORD	Collected Stories
1971	*No Award*	
1972	Wallace STEGNER	Angle of Repose
1973	Eudora WELTY	The Optimist's Daughter
1974	*No Award*	
1975	Michael SHAARA	The Killer Angels
1976	Saul BELLOW	Humboldt's Gift
1977	*No Award*	
1978	James Alan McPHERSON	Elbow Room
1979	John CHEEVER	The Stories of John Cheever
1980	Norman MAILER	The Executioner's Song
1981	John Kennedy TOOLE	A Confederacy of Dunces
1982	John UPDIKE	Rabbit is Rich
1983	Alice WALKER	The Color Purple
1984	William KENNEDY	Ironweed
1985	Alison LURIE	Foreign Affairs
1986	Larry McMURTRY	Lonesome Dove
1987	Peter TAYLOR	A Summons to Memphis
1988	Toni MORRISON	Beloved
1989	Anne TYLER	Breathing Lessons
1990	Oscar HIJUELOS	The Mambo Kings Play Songs of Love
1991	John UPDIKE	Rabbit at Rest
1992	Jane SMILEY	A Thousand Acres

ROMANTIC NOVELISTS' ASSOCIATION MAJOR AWARD

Established in 1960 the award, now sponsored by Boots the Chemists is for the best romantic novel of the year.

	Year	Author	Title
joint winners	1970	Margaret MADDOCKS	Thea
joint winners	1970	Joanne MARSHALL	Cat on a Broomstick
joint winners	1970	Rona RANDALL	Broken Tapestry
	1971	Joanne MARSHALL	Flower of Silence
	1972	Maynah LEWIS	The Pride of Innocence
	1973	Constance HEAVEN	The House of Kuragin
	1974	Frances MURRAY	The Burning Lamp
	1975	Jay ALLERTON	Vote for a Silk Gown
	1976	Anna GILBERT	The Look of Innocence
	1977	Anne WORBOYS	Every Man a King
	1978	Madeleine BRENT	Merlin's Keep
	1979	Josephine EDGAR	Countess
	1980	Joanna TROLLOPE	Parson Harding's Daughter
	1981	Gwendoline BUTLER	The Red Staircase
	1982	Valerie FITZGERALD	Zemindar
	1983	Eva IBBOTSON	Magic Flutes
	1984	Sheila WALSH	A Highly Respectable Marriage
	1985	Rosie THOMAS	Sunrise
	1986	Brenda JAGGER	A Song Twice Over
	1987	Marie JOSEPH	A Better World Than This
	1988	Audrey HOWARD	The Juniper Bush
	1989	Sarah WOODHOUSE	The Peacock's Feather
	1990	Reay TANNAHILL	Passing Glory
	1991	Susan KAY	Phantom
	1992	June KNOX-MAWER	Sandstorm
	1993	Cynthia HARROD-EAGLES	Emily

IAN ST. JAMES AWARDS

Founded in 1989 the annual award is open to writers of short stories. Winners are included in the Annual Collection published by Harper Collins. First prize winners - all short stories.

1989	David ROSE	An Ugly Night
1990	Annie HEDLEY	Mothering Sunday
1991	Faith ADDIS	Small Beginnings
1992	Jeremy CAIN	Black Sky at Night

SUNDAY EXPRESS BOOK OF THE YEAR AWARD

Initiated in 1987 the prize is awarded annually to the author of an outstanding new work of fiction, including short stories, which is first published in English in Britain. No entries are accepted from authors or publishers. Nominations are made by a panel.

1987	Brian MOORE	The Colour of Blood
1988	David LODGE	Nice Work
1989	Rose TREMAIN	Restoration
1990	J.M. COETZEE	The Age of Iron
1991	Michael FRAYN	A Landing on the Sun
1992	Hilary MANTEL	A Place of Greater Safety

BETTY TRASK AWARDS

Started in 1984 and administered by the Society of Authors, the awards are for the benefit of young authors (under 35) and are given on the strength of the manuscript of a first novel of a romantic or traditional rather than experimental nature. The winners are required to use the money for foreign travel. The principal winners are:-

	Year	Author	Title
joint winners	1984	Ronald FRAME	Winter Journey
	1984	Clare NONHEBEL	Cold Showers
	1985	Susan KAY	Legacy
	1986	Tim PARKS	Tongues of Flame
	1987	James MAW	Hard Luck
	1988	Alex MARTIN	The General Interruptor
	1989	Nigel WATTS	The Life Game
	1990	Robert McLiam WILSON	Ripley Bogle
	1991	Amit CHAUDHURI	A Strange and Sublime Address
	1992	Liane JONES	The Dream Stone
	1993	Mark BLACKABY	You'll Never be Here Again *(not yet published)*

WHITBREAD BOOK OF THE YEAR AND LITERARY AWARDS

Established in 1971, five categories of book are now rewarded by Whitbread & Co. These are Novel; First Novel; Children's Novel; Poetry and Biography. Writers must have been resident in Great Britain or the Republic of Ireland for three years or more. Nominations are selected by the panel of judges from each category and one of the category winners is then voted Whitbread Book of The Year. The awards are administered by the Booksellers Association.

	1971	Gerda CHARLES	The Destiny Waltz
	1972	Susan HILL	The Bird of Night
	1973	Shiva NAIPAUL	The Chip Chip Gatherers
	1974	Iris MURDOCH	The Sacred and Profane Love Machine
	1975	William McILVANNEY	Docherty
	1976	William TREVOR	The Children of Dynmouth
	1977	Beryl BAINBRIDGE	Injury Time
	1978	Paul THEROUX	Picture Palace
	1979	Jennifer JOHNSTON	The Old Jest
'Book of The Year'	1980	David LODGE	How Far Can You Go?
	1981	Maurice LEITCH	Silver's City
First Novel	1981	William BOYD	A Good Man in Africa
	1982	John WAIN	Young Shoulders
First Novel	1982	Bruce CHATWIN	On the Black Hill
	1983	William TREVOR	Fools of Fortune
First Novel	1983	John FULLER	Flying to Nowhere
	1984	Christopher HOPE	Kruger's Alp
First Novel	1984	James BUCHAN	A Parish of Rich Women

WHITBREAD BOOK OF THE YEAR AND LITERARY AWARDS (cont.)

	1985	Peter ACKROYD	Hawksmoor
First Novel	1985	Jeanette WINTERSON	Oranges are not the Only Fruit
'Book of The Year'	1986	Kazuo ISHIGURO	An Artist of the Floating World
First Novel	1986	Jim CRACE	Continent
	1987	Ian McEWAN	The Child in Time
First novel	1987	Francis WYNDHAM	The Other Garden
	1988	Salman RUSHDIE	The Satanic Verses
First Novel & 'Book of The Year'	1988	Paul SAYER	The Comforts of Madness
	1989	Lindsay CLARKE	The Chymical Wedding
First Novel	1989	James Hamilton PATERSON	Gerontius
'Book of The Year'	1990	Nicholas MOSLEY	Hopeful Monsters
First Novel	1990	Hanif KUREISHI	The Buddha of Suburbia
	1991	Jane GARDAM	The Queen of the Tambourine
First Novel	1991	Gordon BURN	Alma Cogan
	1992	Alasdair GRAY	Poor Things
First Novel & 'Book of The Year'	1992	Jeff TORRINGTON	Swing Hammer Swing!

YORKSHIRE POST BOOK OF THE YEAR AWARD

An annual award for the book, either fiction or non-fiction, which, in the opinion of the judges, is the best work published in the preceding year.

1970	Edna O'BRIEN	Pagan Place
1971	Paul SCOTT	Towers of Silence
1972	Margaret DRABBLE	Needle's Eye
1973	Evelyn ANTHONY	The Occupying Power
1974	Kingsley AMIS	Ending Up
1975	David LODGE	Changing Places
1976	Nina BAWDEN	Afternoon of a Good Woman
1977	Olivia MANNING	Danger Tree
1978	Sian JAMES	Yesterday
1979	Jennifer JOHNSTON	Old Jest
1980	Anthony BURGESS	Earthly Powers
1981	Paul THEROUX	Mosquito Coast
1982	Elizabeth Jane HOWARD	Getting it Right
1983	Francis KING	Act of Darkness
1984	Kingsley AMIS	Stanley and the Women
1985	Alice Thomas ELLIS	Unexplained Laughter
1986	*No Award to Fiction*	
1987	*No Award to Fiction*	
1988	William TREVOR	The Silence in the Garden
1989	*No Award to Fiction*	
1990	*No Award to Fiction*	
1991	*No Award to Fiction*	
1992	*No Award to Fiction*	

BIBLIOGRAPHY

The books in this short list should be readily available in most public libraries. Together they form an invaluable complement to ***Who Else Writes Like ... ?*** and will help the user find specific authors or titles, pursue the reading of a series, enjoy exploring a particular genre or discover novels set in a particular place or period of history.

In addition to these published titles many libraries now issue excellent local guides to fiction. Always remember to ask the library staff who will be pleased to help.

BLOOMSBURY GOOD READING GUIDE; by Kenneth McLeish.
Bloomsbury Publishing Ltd., 2nd revised ed., 1991.

Contains articles on some 320 authors describing the type of books they write - listing titles and suggesting alternative and 'follow-up' authors and titles.

BLOOMSBURY GOOD READING GUIDE TO MURDER, CRIME FICTION AND THRILLERS; by Kenneth and Valerie McLeish.
Bloomsbury Publishing Ltd., 1990.

Describes the work of 250 crime and thriller writers and suggests follow-up reading by the same author and others.

BLOOMSBURY GOOD READING GUIDE TO SCIENCE FICTION AND FANTASY; by M.H. Zool.
Bloomsbury Publishing Ltd, 1989.

An invaluable complement to the other guides in the series.

CHAMBERS FICTION FILE; compiled and edited by Roger Prebble.
Chambers, 1992.

Divided into three fully cross-referenced sections - authors, titles and characters. Covers over 1,000 authors, over 10,000 novels and over 2,000 characters.

CRIME AND MYSTERY - THE 100 BEST BOOKS, by H.R.F. Keating.
Xanadu, 1987.

Arranged chronologically from Edgar Allen Poe (1845) to P.D. James (1986): these short essays are one person's authoritative and entertaining choice.

CUMULATED FICTION INDEX; Association of Assistant Librarians.

1945-1960	by G.B. Cotton and Alan Glencross
1960-1969	by Raymond Smith
1970-1974	by Raymond Smith and Anthony J. Gordon
1975-1979	by Marilyn E. Hicken
1980-1989	by Marilyn E. Hicken

Taken together this series indexes the majority of novels published in the United Kingdom since the end of the Second World War. The choice of headings continues to be based on the scheme devised by Cotton and Glencross. It would be particularly helpful to readers looking for crime fiction as the index divides this genre into fifteen groups. This series of cumulations is supplemented by Annual Volumes.

DICTIONARY OF LITERARY PSEUDONYMS: A SELECTION OF POPULAR MODERN WRITERS IN ENGLISH; by Frank Atkinson.
The Library Association, 4th revised ed., 1987.

Contains over 6,000 pen names of British and American authors of the twentieth century. Arranged in two sections: real names with pen names added, then pen names with reference to the real name.

AN ENGLISH LIBRARY; edited by Nigel Farrow, Brian Last and Vernon Pratt.
Gower Publishing Co. Ltd. with The Book Trust, 6th ed., 1990.

First published in 1943, the first five editions were edited by F. Seymour Smith. Its objective is to identify the books from the classical and modern heritage that will extend the enjoyment of reading. Nearly 250 writers of adult fiction are included with lists of their most significant works.

HORROR - 100 BEST BOOKS; edited by Stephen Jones and Kim Newman.
Xanadu, 1988.

These one hundred titles have been chosen by current leading horror writers who were invited to nominate their own choice of best books in this genre.

MURDER IN PRINT: A GUIDE TO TWO CENTURIES OF CRIME FICTION; edited by Melvyn Barnes.
Barn Owl Books, 1986.

Illustrates the development of the genre by a selection of almost 500 titles chosen to represent the best examples of the work of 260 writers. A personal selection by an acknowledged expert in the field.

THE NOVELS OF WORLD WAR TWO: AN ANNOTATED BIBLIOGRAPHY OF WORLD WAR TWO FICTION; edited by Michael Paris.
The Library Association, 1990.

Lists over 2,000 novels published in English and in translation from September 1939 to 1988. Arranged in four parts:- (1) Chronological list with annotations; (2) Subject index; (3) Author index; (4) Title index.

NOW READ ON: A GUIDE TO CONTEMPORARY POPULAR FICTION; by Mandy Hicken and Ray Prytherch.
Gower Publishing Co. Ltd., 1990.

This is a similar publication to the Bloomsbury Guide but is arranged in nineteen different genres of fiction. It gives short biographies of the principal authors included and lists their books' titles.

A READER'S GUIDE TO SCIENCE FICTION; by Baird Searles and others.
Facts on File, 1980.

Although now over thirteen years old this book is an excellent introduction to the genre. The largest section describes 200 writers and their work recommending alternative authors 'who write like...'

SEQUELS. VOL. 1: ADULT BOOKS; compiled by Marilyn E. Hicken.
The Association of Assistant Librarians, 10th revised ed., 1992.

Lists novels in which the same characters appear; sequences of novels connected by theme; sequences of novels with a geographical or historical connection; and non-fiction, mainly autobiographical, which is intended to be read in sequence. The arrangement is primarily under the author with an index of series and characters.

TWENTIETH-CENTURY CRIME AND MYSTERY WRITERS; edited by Lesley Henderson. Gale Research International Ltd., 3rd ed., 1991.

Provides detailed information on more than 700 English language writers of mystery fiction including biographical and bibliographical information together with a signed critical essay.

TWENTIETH-CENTURY ROMANCE AND HISTORICAL WRITERS; edited by Lesley Henderson. Gale Research International Ltd., 2nd ed., 1990.

This new edition has been broadened to include historical fiction writers as well as writers of romance. A good, concise reference tool to the genre.

TWENTIETH-CENTURY SCIENCE FICTION WRITERS; edited by Paul E. Schellinger. Gale Research International Ltd., 3rd ed., 1991.

Over 600 writers are represented - ranging from the traditional favourites to the most recent novelists who have altered the style and parameters of this constantly evolving genre.

TWENTIETH-CENTURY WESTERN WRITERS; edited by James Vinson. Gale Research International Ltd., 2nd ed., 1991.

More than 450 entries are included in this edition, chosen to reflect the current state of this complex and diverse genre.

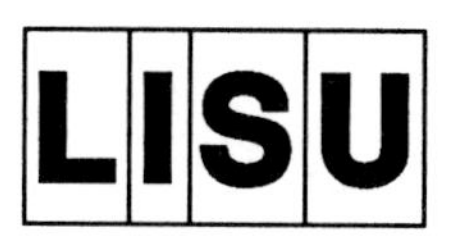

STRATEGIC AIMS

1. LISU'S primary aim is to act as the UK national centre for the collation, analysis and dissemination of statistical data relating to library and information activities.

2. In pursuit of this aim, LISU will, wherever appropriate, work in co-operation with other individuals and organisations in the library, information and book trade communities.

3. If there are significant gaps in the statistical information available, LISU will examine these with a view to initiating or assisting in the collection of data required to fill such gaps.

4. LISU also aims to fill gaps in the supply of trade and general statistics to librarians and other information workers to meet their needs.

5. LISU will provide information and advice to librarians on statistical sources.

6. LISU aims to develop and encourage good practice in librarians' knowledge and use of statistics.

7. LISU aims to act as a source of statistical information on the features of libraries and other information work for people outside the profession (particularly those in the book trade, specialist journalists, and politicians).

8. LISU will, where appropriate, undertake or initiate research projects in connection with any of these aims.

9. LISU will, where appropriate, examine and analyse statistics of library and book trade operations abroad to compare with the British position.

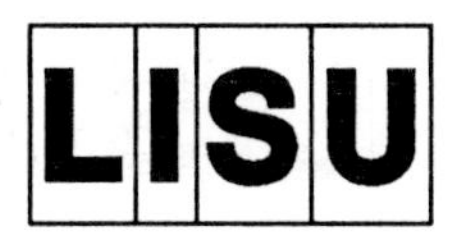

REGULAR PUBLICATIONS

The ***Academic Book Price Index*** publications are always eagerly anticipated and most are supplied against standing orders. These come twice a year in February and early August. They give detailed analysis of price changes by subject category for USA and for UK publications.

The ***Public Library Bookfund Estimates*** was an annual publication (LIBTRAD) listing, for UK authorities, the latest budget projections for spending on books - with previous year's figures. This is now published annually in June as ***UK Public Library Materials Fund & Budget Survey.*** Coverage has been extended to Audio and Video material and to Service Points, Opening Hours and Staffing Levels. Comparisons are presented between individual authorities that respond to the survey.

The main annual publication is the ***LISU Annual Library Statistics - featuring trend analysis of UK academic and public libraries***. Data covers the last ten years, based on returns to CIPFA, UFC and COPOL, supplemented by special enquiries to achieve completeness. National and sector trends and averages are established. This book of 170-180 pages also contains miscellaneous statistical data - useful for librarians to have under one cover - including Prices Indexes, Conversion formulae, Book Trade Statistics, and PLR data on popular authors and book types.

The ***Survey of Public Library Services to Schools and Children in the UK*** is now established as an annual publication. The analysis is based on a questionnaire survey carried out with guidance from AMDECL, SOCCEL and other groups of specialist librarians. There are eleven tables of detailed information by authority with explanatory comments including Per Capita indicators and performance ratios.

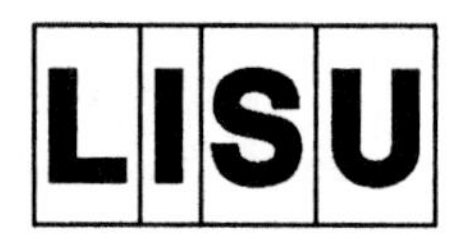

NEW RESEARCH REPORTS (1993)

Practical Performance Indicators 1992, 188 pp. documents the Audit Commission's Citizens' Charter consultation exercise conducted in 1992. It details Proposals, Consultation Responses, and current developments along with a selection of examples of performance measures, management statistics and user surveys from selected UK public library authorities. This composite publication aims to spread the word on interesting and typical management practice.

John Sumsion, ***Report on Statistical Pilot Survey of UK Special Libraries***, 77 pp. Commissioned by the Library Association and Council of Academic and Professional Publishers, this Report demonstrates the problems in defining and surveying so wide a field as all special libraries. Alternative definitions and coverage are discussed and recommendations made. The need for a comprehensive Directory of Libraries, along with statistical content, is considered. Some features of book supply to special libraries are analysed in the response data.

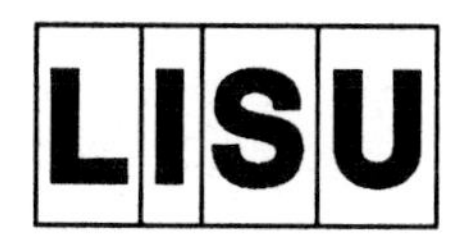